BREAKTHROUGH!

HOW TO GET HIRED IN TODAY'S TOUGH JOB MARKET

FEATURING INNOVATIVE TOOLS THAT RESULT IN MORE INTERVIEWS AND BETTER JOB OFFERS

JAY R. LANG

This publication is designed to provide competent and reliable information regarding the the subject matter covered. However, it is sold with the understanding that the author and published are not engaged in rendering legal, financial, or other professional advice. If legal advice or other expert assistance is required, the services of a professional should be sought.

Published by JETLAUNCH
www.jetlaunch.net

Visit our websites:
www.breakthroughjobcoach.com
www.mobile.twitter.com/btjobcoach
Facebook.com/Breakthroughjobcoach

ISBN: 978-1-944878-08-5

Disclaimer: The views expressed here are solely those of the author in his private capacity and do not in any way represent the views of SUNY Orange, or any institutions, corporations, or living entities.

CONTENTS

PART I: UNEMPLOYMENT—STEALING YOUR PROFESSIONAL IDENTITY

PART II: MARKETING MATERIALS—
HELPING COMPANIES HELP YOU

PART III: POWERFUL TOOLS TO
LEVERAGE YOUR JOB SEARCH

PART IV: THE INTERVIEW AND
THE OFFER

PART V: TIPS AND STRATEGIES
THAT MAKE THE JOURNEY EASIER

PART VI: THE BEGINNING OF A GREAT ADVENTURE

This book is dedicated with love and affection
to all my children, to whom the future belongs.

The more aware you become, the more you shed from
day to day what you have learned so that your
mind is always fresh and uncontaminated
by previous conditioning.

Bruce Lee

Life is good. Stay cool.

Harold D. Lang

IN APPRECIATION

A book of this nature could never have been written alone. I want to thank all those who attended the Job Club and the giving of their time and stories, from which so much of this book was derived; you all know who you are.

Special heartfelt thanks to Sharon Woll. If not for her this book may never have been completed. She was the warrior and proofreader that kept me inspired and dedicated to the book and the 'Breakthough methodology'.

I would also like to thank my business partner in Australia Michael Dryga, and Hope Godcheux, Jessica Guilfoyle, Linda Dunbar, Fritz Kraai, Don Karl, Mike Smith, Frank Annunziata, Bob Ketterer, Dan Donohue, Alfred Perreca, Mary Zak, Hank Spangler, Jules Egyud, and Judy Lekoski-Uurich for their contributions, input and materials. A special thanks to Buddy Norwood and Edward Rapoza for their exceptional mentoring in the 'art' of business. Many thanks to Stephen Knob of Orange County Employment and Training for funding the Job Club program. Special thanks to Lou DeFeo and David Kohn for their faith in the Job Search Networking

Group and SUNY Orange, through the Continuing and Professional Education Department (C.A.P.E.)

I would like to thank my wife for believing in this project and her patience in the hundreds of hours it took to write this book.

Finally I would like to thank my son Jake for giving me the inspiration to write this book and to launch the Breakthrough methodology.

FOREWORD

No one chooses to embark on the bleak road of the unemployed ... the sinking "What do I do now?" feeling. If you find yourself in this place, you need no longer look for an answer. Picking up and embracing the concepts of this book will transform your life forever—launching your life into a positive life trajectory.

I know.

I was 66 years old, recently laid off by a prominent insurance company in Manhattan, and now facing New York unemployment's daunting job search requirements.

I quickly exhausted the department run seminars on resume writing, networking, etc. During the last session, the instructor casually mentioned "Jay's Job Club." It convened twice a week at the Unemployment Compensation building and attendance would meet 2 of 3 of my weekly job search requirements.

Why not?

I first met Jay Lang on January 28, 2014. The Job Club, a group of about 20 individuals comprised an assortment of vocations: musician, accountant, photographers, human resource manager, CEO, building project manager, contractor, nurse, marketing executive, grant writer, business executive. The Job Club which is open to all job seekers, met twice a week, for two hour sessions, and was led by Jay, a recruiter and career counselor well known throughout the northeast.

I was warmly greeted by the group as if I were a prospective member of a Sunday School class. During the first few sessions, I quietly sat, took notes and immersed myself into the content being presented by Jay, as he outlined his non-traditional methods of the job search. I basked in the warmth of my new community of the unemployed. The Job Club, rather than being a down and out group of the discouraged unemployed, had the aura of a book club – we met regularly, had assignments and looked forward to the next meeting with our friends.

During the six months of attending classes, I realized that my life was being transformed. Jay introduced innovative and original tools and techniques to:

- Mitigate a negative mindset. (I call it "putting on my Jay hat")
- Powerfully and proactively approach the job search endeavor in innovative ways
- Take control of the agenda during a job interview with confidence

- Embrace and own my responsibility in the job search mission

This book was conceived within the context of "The Job Club." Here Jay Lang plots out a practical roadmap to the unemployed for successfully securing job interviews and ultimately landing a great job.

He challenges many traditional and widely upheld job search methods as being antiquated, obsolete and actually keeping people unemployed. He debunks common notions of the job search and introduces practical alternative tools and techniques.

To highlight the thesis in his book:

- Millions of unemployed professionals are thrown into a world foreign to them
- The traditional, almost sacrosanct resume hinders, rather than helps, the job search
- Companies are NOT in the business of hiring people and are inept at it

Jay has created and implemented an alternative, revolutionary methodology used in concert with powerful job seeking tools. The results consistently demonstrate the author's ability to help transform individuals into professional job seekers.

From the start Jay engages the reader by identifying with the job seeker's angst and immediately addresses the need for the job seeker to reclaim his professionalism. Even a former CEO of a Fortune 500 company may find himself emotionally paralyzed and unable to take a first step.

The roadmap provided in this book includes three non-conventional tools which give the job seeker a significant competitive advantage:

- The Professional Profile
- The Skills Alignment Matrix
- The Compensation Grid

Another major theme developed in the book is identifying and communicating directly with decision makers at the prospective employer. This circumvents the gatekeepers—Human Resources—and gets the job seeker directly in touch with those with the authority to hire.

The end goal of the job seeker is securing the face to face interview with the prospective employer, acing the interview, and then obtaining a job offer. The mindset includes realizing that every interview question is the candidate's stage in which to shine by putting on full display his amazing accomplishments and telling real life, memorable stories that captivate and compel the interviewer.

Embracing the multidimensional principles presented in this book will provide a fresh competitive edge to any job seeker over most other candidates who are still mired down in the traditional and obsolete job search tools of the past. The strategies outlined in this book put the candidate, not others, in charge of his job search destiny.

By strategically and creatively approaching the job search, you will mitigate the negative mindset, proactively approach prospective employers, take control of the agenda during a job interview, and find yourself energized throughout the process.

So what are you waiting for? Pick up this book and launch yourself into your own life adventure, as I did!

Sharon T. Woll, CPCU
State Filings Manager
Crum & Forster
Morristown, New Jersey

INTRODUCTION

I was facilitating a job search support group in New York when I asked a group of attendees how they felt about losing their jobs, being unemployed and about today's job search.

"I was more nervous about losing my job than I was about getting open heart surgery!" said a former IT sales executive from Manhattan. "And I should know, I had one two years ago!"

"I think everyone should have to go through this hell at least once" said another. "This is the most stressful and humiliating experience I've ever been through. I haven't been without a job in 20 years!"

"I'm at a loss," chimed in a downsized accountant. "I got 2 interviews in the first 2 weeks, now it's been 3 months, 40 some resumes sent out and nothing!"

"Are you applying to jobs you are qualified for?" I asked, knowing the answer.

"Are you kidding. I can do the jobs I apply to with my eyes closed! I've sent out over 100 resumes, and been out of work for 14 months. I was Project Manager for one of the largest financial institutions in the world for 26 years; now I can't even get a phone call!"

I wasn't surprised to hear this at all. In fact, I'd been hearing it since 2009, and it was only getting worse. And, even if the economy had picked up over the years, and the 'official' unemployment rate had fallen to some 5%, there was something seriously wrong with the fact that highly talented professionals were not even getting interviews, let alone jobs.

The Traditional Job Search is Dead

Before the Great Recession, searching for a job wasn't much of a problem. Perhaps you'd never even been unemployed, or if you were, it was a short transitory time and you were back to work within weeks. Now? Weeks have become months and you might even have broken the one year anniversary. Or even worse, 2 or 3 years. You're part of the 'long term unemployed' and all seems hopeless.

How many more times do you tweak your resume? Revise your cover letter? Spend another 2 hours filling out their useless application that only mimics your resume to get no response at all? And when you do get an interview, you just keep getting passed up by someone else.

Today's job search has become a mystery novel without a plot. It keeps twisting and changing with seemingly no end in sight. Then just when you think you have it nailed down with an interview, you're sent a rejection letter 2 weeks later, and it starts all over again.

Most things in life result from consequences from our actions. You work hard, you get paid. You exercise, you feel better. You file your taxes, you stay out of trouble.

Yet with the job search, it doesn't work that way. You apply to a job online that is a seemingly perfect match for you. The cover letter you worked on for hours is flawless. The resume you painstakingly crafted is perfect. You send it off with high hopes and full confidence you will get the job, or at least an interview. Instead you hear nothing.

Weeks go by and when you finally receive a rejection notice, you are actually thrilled that you were at least acknowledged by the company. And this continues on for weeks and months, maybe even years.

This Book is Going to Change All That

It's time to turn things around and take matters into your own hands. Time to boldly face companies and *gently* bring them over to your side by offering them alternatives they least expect. Time to educate them on a new and fresh approach to their current hopeless state of inefficiency in the job search process.

With this book your approach to the entire job search will take on a whole new meaning and direction—and you will start to worker smarter, not harder.

No longer will you approach the job search passively and hoping for the best. You will approach it as it is, *a business venture that puts you in charge.*

It will build your confidence and teach you tools that will help you both personally and professionally. From now on you won't be hopelessly wondering *'what should I do?'* instead you will find yourself asking yourself *'which tools should I use?'*

How do we know the methodology works? It's been tested by thousands of job seekers who are now gainfully employed.

The methodology in this book has proven highly effective for older workers, the long term unemployed, those who are still working and wanting to explore other opportunities, the semi-retired, as well as millennials and recent college graduates.

It is a fact in our modern world, there are very few 'permanent' jobs left. With mergers, acquisitions, recessions, etc., job security is rapidly becoming a thing of the past. With the average job lasting 4.6 years according to the Bureau of Labor Statistics it is as important as getting a college diploma that we all become 'professional job seekers'—if we intend to stay employed in an ever changing and competitive world.

And you are not alone. We are here to personally help you throughout the job search process. Call us and/or visit us on our website with any questions and concerns you may have. We know how important support is throughout this process, and we are your partners in this endeavor in 'today's job search'.

Getting the Most From This Book

This book was written with simplicity and ease in mind. The chapters are kept short for a good reason. They are designed to be a launching pad for your own 'professional business acumen' from which to propel your job search endeavor. We suggest you take the tools from this book and recreate them to fit your needs, your profession, your character and style, and in turn create even more powerful strategies to improve the job search process.

To get the most out of this book, I suggest reading the entire book. This will give you the methodology to use the tools effectively and for maximum impact to jumpstart your job search. Then as you move through the job search process, select those chapters that pertain to the activities of the day.

PART I

UNEMPLOYMENT—STEALING YOUR PROFESSIONAL IDENTITY

Unemployment is a thief. It can steal a lifetime of professional identity in a moment's notice. Reclaiming it and retaining it is crucial for success in finding your job.

CHAPTER 1

WHY IS THE JOB SEARCH SO HARD? (IT'S NOT WHAT YOU THINK!)

The Job Seeker

Your jaw is wracked with pain from an abscessed tooth. You need it pulled now!

A stranger offers you a pair of pliers and some gauze and says *"Go for it!"* Would you know where to start? Of course not.

Yet this is precisely what you are expected to do when you find yourself *unemployed...*

Last week you were Marketing Director of a multimillion dollar company; today you find yourself sweating over whether your cover letter is good enough to get through to Human Resources!

Why is this happening? You may be a chemist, an engineer, an accountant, the controller of a Wall Street hedge fund, but *you're not a 'professional job seeker'*.

Just because you're seeking a job, doesn't mean you know how to get a job—though the world we live in assumes you do.

Looking back, you may have had 3 or 4 jobs over the span of your career. Most of them were before the Great Recession that changed everything.

What do you really know about Human Resources? Resumes? Cover letters? Interviewing? Negotiating a salary? Most will admit, not a lot. Almost all will admit, looking for a job is the *last thing in the world they want to do*. Yet there it is, suddenly confronting you. Get a job, and the quicker you can get one, the better!

The Job Search Today

Today's job search requires a whole new set of alternative tools and nonconventional strategies. It requires a new way of looking at the entire job search, and a deep understanding of what's *really going on out there*—behind the fortress like walls companies have built around themselves—to keep you out and to keep you away from actual Decision Makers.

Traditional job search methods, used by millions of job seekers, just aren't working in this world of change, technological innovation and stiff competition. *In fact the traditional job search tools and processes, in many ways, just may be keeping you unemployed!*

The Companies

Companies are NOT in the business of hiring!

Bank of America specializes in handling people's money and assets, not hiring people. Ford is in the automobile business, not the recruiting business.

Hiring people is a very small part of a company's role. It is a necessary evil that is handled by Human Resources whose primary concerns are with policies and procedures, training, benefits, disciplinary procedures, etc., and focused on finding the 'perfect' candidate to hire—*when they find the time to do recruiting.* The majority of Human Resources personnel spend much less time in the hiring process than most people are aware. In millions of companies, Human Resources is one person, wearing a multitude of hats.

Human Resources are not trained in recruiting and generally don't have much time to effectively take on this challenging role. Which is why they use (ATS) Applicant Tracking Systems to screen out as many applicants as possible to decrease their workload, hire short-term contract Talent Acquisition personnel, and 'farm out' jobs to recruiters to help them find more suitable candidates.

Human Resources are not actual decision makers—and many hardly know the 'real needs' of the hiring managers.

To further demonstrate that companies don't understand the hiring process, they demand resumes and applications which are only shreds of a one's career. Documents, which are only *one dimensional* in scope and tell them only what the applicant has done in the past; yet do not relate to the employer's specific needs of today.

Companies report that hiring good people is one of their biggest challenges. According to Stephen Moulton of PR Newswire 46% of new hires totally fail within 18 months.

All of this further creates more challenges to the job seeker; creating more hoops to jump through, more non-decision makers to talk to, and more time and money lost in the job search process.

Yet nothing changes and companies continue to do the same things. They continue to make bad hires and continue to keep great candidates from getting the jobs they deserve. Why do companies continue these practices that hurt both themselves and the job seeker? *They are NOT in the business of hiring.*

The Unemployment Industry

In between all this—the nonprofessional job seeker and the *incompetent at hiring* company—is a mountain of technology, redundant information, and a multibillion dollar industry that profits off your pain, frustration and unemployment. With every day you are unemployed, with every click of your mouse, every resume you sent out, every job site you scan, money is being made; billions of it—and it's not going into your pocket. The selling of your information is big business—and, by the nature of it, it's also keeping you unemployed, and keeping *you* unemployed, keeps them in business.

What can you you do about it?

By understanding *why is it so hard,* you can begin the process of becoming a *professional* in a job search mode. Once you begin to see the weaknesses of companies in hiring, you will approach the job search in an entirely new way. You will start using tools that generate more interviews and better offers. Your mindset will be in a proactive, strategic and business oriented mode. You will find yourself in a stronger position to leverage your expertise and professionalism. The process will become easier, less tedious and far more productive than you ever thought possible. You will begin to think smarter, not work harder. And, you will start to think for yourself, as a professional does—not just keep doing what 'they' tell you to do, to get a job. In fact, you may even begin to enjoy the job search process. So relax, and get ready to help companies help you get back to work!

CHAPTER 2

RECLAIM YOUR PROFESSIONALISM AND RECLAIM YOUR JOB

When you had the company name behind you—the office, business cards, your weekly compensation—you never questioned your professionalism.

If you had a crisis at work, you'd pick up the phone and get it resolved. If you needed to talk to the boss, you'd do it. If you lost that deal, you'd focus on what you had in your pipeline to keep the money rolling in. All your education, on-the-job training, and years of work experience created your sense of professional identity. You knew what to do, how to do it, and who to deal with to get the job done.

Then you lost your job. Now, self-doubt is creeping in. You're losing your sense of focus. You're experiencing anger, bitterness and depression. You're becoming highly emotional over the process, and you're beginning to realize it is not as easy as you once thought.

You are also starting to question nearly everything you do: the resumes you create, the cover letters you write, what to say in an interview. The thought of picking up the phone and calling a Decision Maker at a company now fills you with dread.

You are in a crisis mode. What do you do now? What have you been doing?

When you were working, you wouldn't even consider contacting Human Resources to solve your problems. Now? In the midst of a business and personal crisis—no income, no book of business, no clients, no customers, no benefits—you are suddenly doing everything you can to grasp after Human Resources; going to *non-Decision Makers* to help you with your crisis.

Why is this happening? *You have allowed unemployment to steal your professional identity.* Your *business as usual* state of mind has been replaced with emotions, anxiety and fear. Some have equated it to having a stroke, where suddenly even the simplest of tasks are arduous.

You must *reclaim* your professionalism. You must realize that your skills and competence have not suddenly vanished with the loss of your job. That all the years of education, on the job training, and experience have not suddenly evaporated into thin air. They are still there, you just need to take them back. Start thinking like the professional you always have been. *Start doing everything as if you were still employed.* Again: *Start doing everything as if you were employed!* Reclaim the professional that you are and stop allowing unemployment to steal your professional identity.

CHAPTER 3

THE CLOAK OF BITTERNESS—
THE ANGER THAT KEEPS
YOU UNEMPLOYED

Anger, bitterness and resentment due to the loss of one's job, may be the biggest hurdle to get over once you begin your job search. Get over it and all your energy can be focused in a positive beam to success. Hold onto it, and it will hold you back, drag you down, alienate you, and keep you unemployed.

After a workshop I was talking to a new attendee who hadn't said much during the session. I asked him what he'd been doing, what had happened to his last job.

"It was a great job! Great group of people, good money and I was there for three years. Then one Monday a few months ago they called all of us in and told us to pack our stuff as they were letting everyone go. That the business couldn't make it as is and that they were sorry. Period."

"I'm sorry that happened, but how do you feel about that?"

"I'm mad as hell at them. That's how I'm feeling. I loved that job!"

"Wait a minute. Did that job pay for your mortgage? Put food on your table? Heat your home and put gas in your car?"

"Yea" he replied, trying to figure out where I was going.

"Then it ran into hard times and had to let you go, right?"

"Yea, but ..."

"Wait a second, hear me out here. If you think about it, they totally fulfilled their obligation. The deal was, you work hard for them and they paid you money. Then due to circumstances they fell on hard times and had to let you go. To *them* it was a *business transaction pure and simple.* They paid you when they needed you and let you go when they didn't."

Then I asked him "So why are you making this personal? Wasn't it just a business transaction.?"

He nodded his head and said "You're right."

This same situation is played out over and over in our workshops. Anger, bitterness and resentment at one's previous company for being let go. In fact if allowed, the workshops could easily become one long 'bitch' session. Yet when we look at the relationship between the two parties, employer and employee, we can see it is nothing more than just a business transaction. (Although we love to convince ourselves it was much more).

"I gave 30 years of my life to that company!" An ex IBM employee expressed. Yes, 30 years of your life where you *chose* to give your time, energy and expertise for exchange for a very nice compensation package. Now you are angry at them for letting you go?

Of course there are unfair dismissals. Layoffs due to age discriminations, etc., yet in the end, if it leaves you months or even years later feeling angry, the only one you are hurting is yourself—and in seeking a job, it can hurt you a lot more than just emotionally.

This is where the cloak of bitterness comes in. No matter how hard you try to hide your anger, it's still there and will come up to haunt you. It hangs on you like an ugly old cloak.

Countless times job seekers will tell me they can hide it. That they would never display this disdain towards their old company during an interview. But they're only fooling themselves. If you're full of resentment, it will inevitably surface and it just may be keeping you unemployed.

If you find yourself wrapped in the cloak of bitterness, it's vital you remove it as soon as possible. In the workshops we figuratively ask all attendees to remove it and place it on the hanger in the closet of bitterness. Shed the cloak of bitterness; it is an encumbrance that impedes your progress towards the goal.

This simple act, a decision you choose to make, has become one of the most memorable and helpful exercises of the workshops. People has countlessly exclaimed how important this was in their job search. How crucial it was to finally getting themselves into a professional mind-set and back to a clear mind that was looking *forward* to great things instead of looking *back* to their last company and only feeling angry.

Remember, your previous relationship was simply a business transaction. It has ended and now is the time to reclaim your professionalism, look forward, leave the cloak of bitterness behind, and move ahead and concentrate on a new business transaction that may be just around the corner.

CHAPTER 4

ME, INC.—THE MINDSET THAT PUTS *YOU* IN CONTROL

The moment you lost your last job, you instantly launched a new career with a long list of titles and responsibilities: No matter what your previous role was, your new job is now 'the full time job search'. Finding one buyer for your services.

This involves creating marketing materials, brand building, cold-calling, generating leads, setting appointments, face to face consultations, networking, time management, financial analysis, record keeping, staying abreast of the latest trends in your industry, etc., etc., etc.

Thinking of yourself as a business assists the mind to think like a business. As businesses market their goods and services to you on a daily basis through their various forms of advertising, it's only logical for you to market your services to companies as a business.

Unfortunately the vast majority of job seekers are intimidated by companies. They sit at their computers and passively send out their resumes and cover letters hoping to get a response from the buyer (the company). From a business point of view, this is poor marketing and rarely results in the closing of a sale. Similarly for the job seeker, this is often not an effective strategy for getting a job.

Keep in mind, you only need to find one buyer. Not five, not ten, but one buyer who will compensate you for the services your profession dictates in the market place.

Think of yourself as a business. A business that contracts out your services to companies. You will find yourself being more objective in your approach to the job search, and less intimidated by companies and those you meet and try to contact.

Larry, a Sales Manager had just accepted a $55,000 offer when I met him. He had previously been making $88,000 and was distraught. When questioned why he didn't negotiate higher, he replied "I needed the job and I guess I was intimidated." Then I explained the concept of Me, Inc., asking him afterwards if his decision was good for *his company?* Shaking his head he went away.

A week later Larry returned to the workshop and exclaimed after sitting down "You changed my life!" Now it was my turn to shake my head. "I seriously doubt that" I replied "but tell me about it".

Larry explained that after he left, he realized that his entire working life had been catering to companies on a personal level. *Not on a business level.* "This was a huge eye opener for me, and I decided to make a change. I called up a supplier of the company that had made me the offer, as they were *also* advertising for a Sales Manager and told them I was very interested. I also told them I needed at least $80,000. This time, I wasn't intimidated. I got an interview, and an offer of $80,000! All because of a change in attitude. From now on, I'll always think of myself as a company. Me, Inc!"

So take up the responsibilities of the CEO of your own company and start making those executive decisions now. If it's not good for *your* company, keep working the deal until it is!

CHAPTER 5

BE THE SOLUTION TO THEIR PROBLEM AND WATCH THE POWER SHIFT

The majority of people approach the job search as if they are looking for a job that provides a solution to *their* problem. Does it pay enough? Will it provide a good benefits package? What is the vacation time?

To be successful in your job search, your focus must be away from your needs and on providing a solution to an *employer's* problem.

Are you targeting *their* needs? Do you have the ability to solve *their* problems?

If you breakdown the whole process of why employers hire people, it comes down to one very basic fact. They have a problem, a need, and they hire people to solve it. Simple as that. Yet, a difficult concept to grasp when all we think about is ourselves.

Now take a look at your current 'marketing materials', that is your resume and cover letter. Are they providing a solution to an employer's problems? Do they succinctly demonstrate that you are the answer to their needs? Or are they all about you? More than likely, they will revolve entirely around you. Why? Because more than likely you are using the traditional resume and cover letter. *More about that later.*

Consistently across the board, job seekers watch their number of interviews to resumes sent out increase, and those interviews turn to jobs when they concentrate on being the solution to the employer's problem. A shift of power—that is by addressing their needs, your needs get met!

When your focus is on providing solutions to an employer's problems, you also become more strategic and more proactive. You impress hiring authorities and put yourself ahead of the other candidates—putting you in a position to get more interviews and better offers.

CHAPTER 6

THE BUSINESS TRANSACTION—WHEN OUR EMOTIONS RULE, WE LOSE

As long as we let our emotions rule in the job search, we're in trouble. Emotions impede the job search process, fluster our ability to think clearly, and in turn put us in a state of being out of touch with our professionalism. Emotions are our enemy, and we must learn to put them aside in our job search endeavors.

Maintaining the mindset that the job search, and in essence the job itself, is simply a business transaction, that an employer has a need to fulfill, and your job is to clearly communicate you are the solution to their needs, will keep you focused on the business of a professional job search. This in turn can help to control your emotions and helps to ward off desperation and anxiety.

When Netflix decided to change their pricing strategy in 2011, their stocks plummeted and their customer base eroded, practically overnight. Did Reed Hastings, CEO and Co-founder let his emotional response dictate his plan of action? No. He got to work on how to remedy a bad business decision. That's what professional business people do.

In the same way, when you apply for a job, go to an interview, talk to someone about 'opportunities', and all other endeavors in the *professional* job search, shift your focus away from your emotional concerns to their needs, maintaining at all times it's a business transaction and should be treated as such.

As you move through this book, you will pick up 'tools' that will help you maintain this state of mind, and increase your confidence. It's one thing to tell someone to not be emotional, especially during a time of great emotional upheaval. However, it's another thing to provide in essence a toolbox, filled with tools that can help alleviate the anxiety when it arises. Start collecting them and using them as you move through the job search. You will find your confidence rising and your damaging emotions dissipating as you zone in on the true nature of the job search; filling needs and demonstrating to employers how your skills and experience can solve their problems.

CHAPTER 7

TURNING THE JOB SEARCH INTO A MARKETING CAMPAIGN

It is impossible to overestimate the power of marketing. Today's job search must be an active endeavor of strategic and effective marketing. Your services are a valuable product, and must be demonstrated as such. The prolific and bestselling author Brian Tracy writes in his bestselling book *Marketing* "In our dynamic, competitive economy, marketing is the core function of every successful enterprise. No matter what business you are in, you are in the "marketing business".

Sustaining a strategic marketing edge and maintaining a marketing mindset will set you apart from the crowd and get you closer to your goal.

It is imperative that every action you perform and every document you create demonstrate this marketing focus. As one unemployed Supply Chain professional in a workshop so accurately proclaimed "No exposure, no promotion, no asking, no returns!"

With that firmly entrenched in our minds, that we are in the "marketing business", the following five (5) chapters will explore powerful, unique tools that will help set you apart from the crowd and get you noticed. Using the tools in the methodology presented will land you more interviews, help you perform at a higher level of thinking to ace those interviews, and ultimately land the job that *you* want.

PART II

MARKETING MATERIALS—
HELPING COMPANIES
HELP YOU

These powerful tools are designed to cut through the quagmire, communicate precisely who you are and what you have to offer, and get you closer to Decision Makers.

CHAPTER 8

THE PROFESSIONAL PROFILE—THE COMPETITIVE ADVANTAGE

The Professional Profile, as it is described, and used in this book, has proven time and time again to be one of the most important tools to increase your ratio of interviews, be seen by Decision Makers and ultimately get you more offers.

The Professional Profile is simply a bullet-pointed list of your *key skills and accomplishments spanning your entire career.* It presents *quantifiable values, measurable accomplishments, verticals, capabilities, and recognizable, iconic names in an easy-to-read and easy to sell format.*

Think of the Getting Started guide that comes along with a 100-page manual for your new cell phone. If you want to start using the phone in the next few minutes, do you read the manual? Most people will begin with the Getting Started guide.

The Professional Profile is brief and provides instant evidence that you are a good candidate for the job, while the resume (like the manual) takes more time to decipher and makes the employer wade through loads of information to try to understand how you meet their needs.

Think of the advantage you will have when your key skills and accomplishments are instantly understood over those other candidates whose materials have to be 'worked through' to even get somewhat of an idea as to what they have to offer.

Let's examine some of the many ways the Professional Profile can help you in your job search:

1. The Professional Profile creates a visual reminder of your *value*. Writing down your talents, skills, accomplishments, key company names, important clients, titles, fortes you possess, etc., is the first step in reclaiming your professionalism and in marketing yourself as the unique and outstanding product you are.

2. It creates perceptions that you can control. There are no dates, no employment gaps, no questionable factors to negatively impact the reader. Unlike the resume, the Professional Profile prevents you being judged by your age, gaps in your employment history, etc.

3. It becomes a 'cheat sheet' you can use while you're on the phone with decision-makers or during a

phone interview. It gives you tangible points for a dialogue that focuses on your value, and how you meet the employer's needs. It's a great stress reliever. When you are asked the dreaded question, *Tell me about yourself,* the Professional Profile helps you stay in control of the conversation.

4. It helps to answer one of the most frequently asked questions by those thinking of changing careers: "What do I really want to do?" By writing down what you have done, and accomplished, you will remember what you have excelled in. You can then begin to see where your previous skills and accomplishments may align with new careers you never considered before.

5. Composing cover letters becomes painless; all the skills and accomplishments that align with the position offered can be cut and pasted straight into your cover letter.

6. A well-written Professional Profile can be pasted into your LinkedIn Profile or any other medium that requires you to show who you are and what you have to offer in a powerful and succinct way.

7. By summarizing your strengths with the needs of the company, it instantly grabs the attention of those seeking the 'right' candidate and launches you into the interviewing stage.

8. The Professional Profile gives recruiters and HR *strong succinct one-liners* that can be lifted from the Profile and used to sell you to hiring managers.

9. It replaces the resume. The Professional Profile has been so successful in getting the attention of decision makers that it has landed a substantial number of job seekers a job without even having submitted a traditional resume.

10. It makes the phone ring. *It is becoming quite the norm that sending out your resume doesn't get results.* Even if you are the 'perfect candidate' Human Resources may not be able to see it. So instead of sending out just resumes on line, send out your Professional Profile as well to a Decision Maker in the company. It often sparks their interest and they want to learn more.

The following are examples of various Professional Profiles. Some are very simple drafts and some more detailed. Customize yours as you see fit.

Notice as you read them, how quickly you are able to 'size up' these candidates. How clearly you can see the value they can bring to an organization. Consider how easily the key skills and accomplishments of the candidates can be passed along in the hiring process. Now make them yours. Keep them lean and powerful. Cut out all the fluff, and bring your amazing Key Skills and Accomplishments to light.

Example 1

Human Resources Manager
Professional Profile

HR Professional with 15 years experience in managing a full spectrum of human resources services.

Key Skills

- HR Manager for union and nonunion
- HR Policies and Procedures
- Staff recruitment and Retention
- Disciplinary Procedures
- Management & Employee training and development
- Mediation/dispute resolution
- Payroll processes
- FMLA/Workers Comp/Disability/FLSA
- Benefits coordinator

Accomplishments

- Hired 300 employees for newly built company within first year of opening
- Cut recruiting time 35% by creating qualification systems and review processes
- Created tax incentives of up to 25% by utilizing HIRE Act
- Generated $40,000 annually by taking advantage of the OJT (on the job training)

- Reduced cost of unemployment insurance through documentation and termination process
- Reduced turnover by up to 75%

Example 2

Sales, Marketing, and Management Professional

Executive Level Leadership | Sales Management Marketing | Capital Management | Mergers and Acquisitions | Integrations | P & L Responsibility | Legal | Contracts | Startup | Turnaround | CRM Systems

Accomplishments

- Start-up - $0 – $25,000,000 in office equipment, supplies, and parts distributing to office equipment dealers throughout U.S. – Sales Manager - Ikon Office Solutions
- Turnaround - $3,000,000 – $18,000,000 Grew parts distributor by expanding lines of product and territory coverage in U.S. and export – Director of Sales
- Managed increase of capital equipment from 17,000 machines to 120,000 in the NY Metro marketplace. $300,000,000 branch. Became largest provider in largest market in U.S. $1.2 billion Company. V.P. of Sales

Key Skills

- Lead successful sales teams. Start-up, Mid-Size, and Fortune 500
- Planned and implemented winning Sales and Marketing strategies

- CRM planning and implementation – Salesforce, Sales Logix, Oracle
- Tradeshows, Networking, Industry events
- New product Development – Sourcing, projections, launch, life cycle
- Contract review, negotiations, approvals and enforcement
- Change management
- Capital management and budgets
- Websites, E-commerce, Social media

Education | M.B.A Management, B.A. Marketing

Example 3

Systems Programmer, Technologist
Professional Profile

Corporate IT Systems Solutions:

- z/OS systems, DR, vendors, network, and automation
- z/VM network and automation
- MS Windows and Linux Desktop connectivity and compliance

Accomplishments:

- Conducted two major zOS release upgrade projects delivered on schedule with NO defects.
- Planned and implemented, as tower lead, 400+ zOS level set software upgrades delivering a 99.75% success.
- IBM Service Excellence Award for emergency security maintenance implemented over the holidays.
- Planned and implemented the zVM/zLinux production and QA network environments with 100% success.
- Successfully navigated the outsourcing and subsequent in sourcing of JPMC entire technical team to/from IBM.
- Supported hundreds of LPAR DR Tests and 3 real DRs; Houston Flood, Florida hurricane

and 9/11 World Trade for which I received the JPMC's Super Star Award.

- Successfully mentored and developed several junior raw recruits to be productive at project levels.
- Technical lead converted SNA mainframe connectivity to 98% IP.

Technology Experience:

- Operating Systems
- zOS 2.1, JES2/NJE, ACF/VTAM, Enterprise Extender, TCP/IP, TELNET, TN3270E, FTP, SMTP, OMPRoute, VIPA, DNS, OMVS; Netview 5.4/REXX/Pipes; Omegamon/XE/VTAM; MQ Series and CICS, ChangeMan ACF2.
- TSO/E, REXX, CLIST, ISPF/PDF, SDSF, RMF, SMP/E, RACF, JCL/Utilities, IPCS, GTF, CTRACE, BAL, SAS
- zVM 5.4, CMS, VSWITCH, TCP/IP, OMPRoute, RSCS, PVM. z/TPF.

Network Products:

- CA NetmasterIP 1.6, TPX, Teleview, Ops/MVS, XCOM; Sterling Connect:Direct 4.8(NDM), Secure+; LRS VPS;

Hardware:

- IBM z12, Gigabit OSA Express, FE-OSA, OSA-2, IP/OSPF, CISCO 7500 router, 5509 Switch, 3x74 controllers.

Desktop and Internet:

- MS W8.1, W7; MS Office Suite, Project, VISIO, Sharepoint, System Center Config Manager(SCCM/2012)
- IBM PComm; Attachmate Extra! X-treme 9.0, Reflections; Rumba; OpenText Host Explorer
- IBMLINK, IGC(Advantis), Google Search(SEO) and Google Products/Services/Cloud Computing.

Employers

NYCT via IIC	Consultant Systems Analyst – Compliance
BOBKET.NET, LLC	Consultant Local SEO Business
CITI via BOBKET.NET, LLC	Consultant z/VM Systems Developer
IBM via CSI	Consultant z/OS Systems Programming
JPMorgan Chase	Sr. Systems Programming/Engineer, Technical Lead
JPMorgan Chase via IBM	Consultant Sr. Systems Management Integration
Insurance Service Office	Lead Network Systems Programmer

Meldisco   Senior Systems
                               Programmer

Comdisco   Consultant Disaster
                               Recovery Engineer

CHAPTER 9

THE RESUME/CV—
HELPING OR HINDERING
YOUR JOB SEARCH?

Are you sending out dozens or perhaps even hundreds of resumes and not getting any results? More than likely your resume is sabotaging your job search.

The resume, no matter how well-written, is a marketing tool that asks an employer:

Guess what I can do for you? *Guess* how I can meet your needs?" *Why?* Because it's all about *you*, it is not about *their* needs.

Think about it for a moment. Imagine a company selling a product that forces the buyer to 'guess' how the product will meet their needs?

Look around you. You know exactly how your smartphone meets your needs. You know exactly how your car meets your needs. But the typical resume?

A resume makes the reader work very hard to understand what you can do, what you have to offer, and most importantly, if and how you can meet the needs of the company.

The resume is not only a poor marketing tool, it will often do more harm than good. Dates can eliminate you in a matter of seconds. You're too old. You're a job-hopper. You can't keep a job. You're unemployed. What's this 6 month gap? How does what you did 5 years ago align with our needs today? Are your skills current?

A typical resume creates perceptions you can't control. At a time when controlling perceptions is crucial, the resume, your #1 marketing tool, often fails. This will often work against even the most qualified candidates.

Of course, due to the demands of the marketplace, resumes are still required by the majority of companies. Therefore since we are usually forced to use them, let's make sure what we provide is powerful, succinct, controlling of perceptions and easily understood for all who receive it.

Today on the market there is a plethora of books on how to write resumes. However, if the following proven formats are used, you can be confident they will work for you, if supplemented with the Professional Profile and the other tools described in in this book.

Chronological vs functional resumes

The two most common resume formats are the chronological (sample 1) and the functional resume (sample 2). The chronological resume lists your previous jobs according to the dates. The functional resume puts the emphasis on your key skills and accomplishments while leaving your list of employers near the end of your resume.

We suggest using the chronological format for those who have recently lost their jobs or are still employed, have a steady work history and their skill sets align well with the jobs they are applying. Keep in mind, employers looking at your resume will primarily see only your most recent accomplishments and skills. Those talents further down the chronological line will probably be skipped over. This is the weakness of this format. You will also be labeled by your last position. With the chronological format it is hard to prevent those bad perceptions which can prevent you from getting interviewed.

The functional format (See Chapter 10) works extremely well with those who has been unemployed for a lengthy period or have gaps of unemployment, wish to change careers, possess a career that is rather nebulous to define, have been underemployed, and perhaps most importantly have issues that may give off bad perceptions that are keeping them from getting interviews.

User friendly and reader friendly

When creating your resume, it is important to create a resume that is both 'User Friendly' and 'Reader Friendly'. The 'User' being you. The 'Reader' being the recipient.

The 'User Friendly' resume allows you to quickly revise it when need be. As all jobs have different needs, it's important to be able to easily edit your resume on the fly. Don't sabotage your ability to apply to a job because you are too 'sick and tired' of revising your resume. Keep it in a simple, user friendly format.

The 'Reader Friendly' resume has bullet points and strong succinct sentences that demonstrate your skills and accomplishments. It's 'easy' to read.

Stay away from paragraphs as much as possible. When a resume is being scanned by Human Resources, recruiters and busy decision makers, your paragraph will more than likely be skimmed over with very little retention by the reader. Make it pleasing to the eye. Hold it up without even reading it, if it looks too challenging, simplify it. Less is more. Keep it reader friendly.

Give it a title. If you are a Corporate Trainer, then title your resume as such. Don't make the reader guess. Be aware that titles change within companies of the same industry. Make sure you are titling your resume to align with the position you are applying. Don't ever assume the recipient can figure it out. Keep it simple and tell them.

A powerful resume uses keywords that align with the needs of the job description. It uses bullet points instead of lengthy paragraphs, and lists minimal responsibilities with lots of exciting accomplishments.

A good resume clearly demonstrates your accomplishments in ways that are quantifiable and target the employer's needs. Don't *tell* me you are *detail-oriented; show* me you "Created a 50 page training manual used in a call center with more than 800 employees." Don't *tell* me you are innovative, *show* me you "Patented a product that is currently on the market and has sold over 5 million units" (Notice the use of numerals over spelling the word out. Numbers are like eye-candy, they stick out, make it easier to read, and are retained by the human mind far more than words.)

Be strategic. *Your goal is to communicate your value in such a way it can easily be seen, retained and passed along to other hiring authorities.*

The **sample 4** below demonstrates a well constructed resume that tells the reader the *candidate's profession*. It keeps the introduction to a minimum.

The *Key Skills and Capabilities* quickly give the reader all the expertise the candidate holds. This format allows the candidate to easily remove or add to the list as a job description requires. These are the keywords that will get you through the Applicant Tracking System (screening software) that search for keywords that either accept you or reject you. It also helps the HR personnel or a recruiter to size you up in a matter of a few seconds.

It then *names the company* and describes what the company does. This can be very helpful, especially if the name of the company is not well known.

Then we start with the bullet points of *very few responsibilities* and a lot of *accomplishments* demonstrated in quantifiable value. These are extremely easy to communicate to third parties. This is an essential quality of any well written resume.

To demonstrate this particular candidate, just by glancing at this resume, a recruiter or HR personnel could easily pick up the phone and describe the candidate as follows:

I have a highly accomplished Senior Level Engineering and Technology leader with experience in software and hardware engineering with extensive Far East manufacturing experience. He is highly competent in Budgeting, cost control, ROI, vendor relations and mergers and acquisitions.

He holds multiple patents and has managed budgets of over $9 million and led teams of 75 on a global basis in the US, Hong Kong, China and Australia.

He has slashed industrial design budgets by 50% and increased corporate margins by 30% while keeping with all product quality and performance metrics.

He is currently looking at opportunities and would like to discuss with you what your needs are and how he may be of assistance to your company.

Example 4

SENIOR-LEVEL ENGINEERING & TECHNOLOGY LEADER

Technology executive with extensive international experience developing and delivering in consumer electronic (CE) products to global markets.

KEY SKILLS AND CAPABILITIES

Software/Hardware Engineering • OEM/ODM/JDM • 3rd-Party & Offshore Development • Vendor Relations • Patent Portfolio Management • Technology Partnerships • Budgeting, Cost Control, ROI, P&L Analysis • Management • Quality Control • Far East Manufacturing • Continuous Lifecycle Process Improvement • Acquisitions and Technical Due Diligence

PROFESSIONAL EXPERIENCE & ACCOMPLISHMENTS

ALTEC LANSING, LLC – Milford, PA   2005-Present

Vice President, Engineering (2009-2011)

- Reporting to the President, co-led ongoing strategic planning and support of corporate carve-out while ensuring consistent product design, development, production, and delivery.
- Managed $6M-$9M budget while directing 45-member worldwide Engineering, Quality, and

Program Management personnel located in the US, Hong Kong, China, and Australia.

- Slashed Industrial Design budget 50% and improved time-to-market by internalizing the ID function.

- Executed strategic transition to 3rd-party and ODM development resulting in 25% reduction in engineering operating expenses while improving development bandwidth.

- Achieved aggressive corporate margin improvement goal of over 30% while simultaneously meeting all product quality and performance metrics by implementing DFC and DFM initiatives.

Senior Director, Engineering (2005-2009)

- Managed $4M-$6M budget, directing 30-member US-based Engineering, Quality, and Program Management teams with additional coordination across Hong Kong/China teams.

- Key contributor to strategic roadmap definition and delivery.

- Maintained productive relationships with multiple strategic partners including Apple, Microsoft, and Sirius/XM.

- Improved time-to-market 20% while increasing development bandwidth by introducing module-based platform strategy, enabling functional modules to be reused across multiple products.

- Established coding standards and code review process, improving team effectiveness/efficiency in delivery of production-ready firmware.

DIGITAL 5, Lawrenceville, NJ   2001-2005
Vice President, Engineering

- Reported to the President, and managed $3M+ budget.
- Directed product development lifecycle from concept through manufacturing.
- Led 15-40 member global teams located in the US, Austria, China, and India.
- Delivered multiple "1st of its kind," award-winning products utilizing wireless networking technologies to reliably distribute audio & video throughout the home.

FRANKLIN ELECTRONIC PUBLISHERS,
Burlington, NJ   1990-2001

Vice President, Software Engineering   (1998-2001)
Director, Software Engineering   (1993-1998)

- Managed $5M-$8M budget.
- Directed all software/firmware operations, leading a staff of 78 diverse technical resources.
- Successfully took 70+ products to market.
- Implemented many proprietary innovative technologies including advanced spell

- Launched Bookman, the industry's 1st e-book reader;

Previous professional experience includes Senior Software Engineer / Product Developer with Franklin Electronic Publishers, and Software Engineer with Advanced System Development, Loral Electronic Systems, and Partner at MLC Associates.

EDUCATION & PATENTS

BS, Computer Science, State University of New York at Stony Brook, Stony Brook, NY

Graduate studies in Computer Science, Polytechnic Institute of New York, White Plains NY

Patent Number 5,007,019 for "Electronic Thesaurus with Access History List" • Patent Number 5,739,451 for a "Hand Held Electronic Music Encyclopedia" • Multiple Additional Patents in Process

Example 5

Name

New City, NY 10956 Cell: xxx.xxx.xxxx email *http://www.linkedin.com*

Sales, Marketing, and Management Professional

Executive Level Leadership | Sales Management | Marketing | Capital Management | Mergers and Acquisitions | Integrations | P & L Responsibility | Legal | Contracts | Startup | Turnaround | CRM Systems | Customer Relationships | Product Development | Vendor Relationships

High performance leader of successful teams in companies sized up to Fortune 500.

- Start-up from $0 - $25,000,000 at office equipment distributor.
- Navigated turnaround of a 23 year old company with declining sales by expanding sales force nationally and internationally and broadening the product line. $3,000,000 to $18,000,000.
- Managed increase of 17,000 machines to 120,000 through organic growth and merger / acquisition in NY Metro. 10,000 accounts with 10 Area Sales Managers. Customers included Property managers, Condo/Coop, Landlords, Developers, Housing agencies, Schools, and Hospitals.

- $300,000,000 + in branch revenue. Brought equipment to 99% coinless and 23% cashless in two years.

CSC Serviceworks, SDI, Yonkers N.Y.   01/2011 – 03/2015

Market Leader Provides Equipment and Services to Multifamily Buildings

V.P. of Sales

- Managed 10,000 accounts and secured 1300 contracts in 2014. $300,000,000 in annual revenue.
- Increased market share 25% through innovative sales strategy.
- Merged 5 companies in 2 years in NY Metro market.
- Led outside sales team of ten to establish eight year contracts, new business and renewal agreements.
- Lead innovation of coinless and cashless laundry rooms utilizing the latest payment and M2M monitoring technologies.
- Reduced account attrition/machine loss by 30% through process improvements. Enforced contract rights and worked toward amicable solutions. Saved 700 machines.
- Managed sales pipeline and account activity through Salesforce.com and Clarify call center software.

Polek and Polek, Fairfield N.J.   06/1997 – 01/2011
Distributed Office equipment Supplies, and Parts

Director of Sales

- Drove business from $3,000,000 to $18,000,000 through organic expansion throughout U.S. and export business.
- P & L Responsibility – Managed by customer, product category, customer, geography, and overall performance. Averaged 20% revenue growth per year at 30 – 35 % gross profit margin.
- Instituted purchase agreements to create monthly sales commitments from customers.
- Over 220 customers gained through "Approved Vendor" status for large industry buying group
- New business development – Managed product life cycle, built pipeline of suspects and prospects based upon market analysis and customer feedback.
- Planned and implemented e-commerce site, driving 30% of business through this channel.

Education: M.B.A. Management, B.S. Marketing—St. Thomas Aquinas College

Networking/Awards/Community – Vistage – Key Executive - 10 years, Business Networking Intl (B.N.I.)

Golden Circle Award four years, Entrepreneurial Spirit Award, IAHD Leadership Committee, President A.O.H.

CHAPTER 10

CHANGING PERCEPTIONS WITH THE FUNCTIONAL PROFESSIONAL PROFILE RESUME

How we are perceived is largely dependent on the materials we present.

If we have 10 years of pharmaceutical sales experience, but our resume states our last job of 3 years was a teller in a bank, then we are perceived as a bank teller. If we have a degree in Marketing, worked with an advertising firm for 5 years, but our resume states our last job was as a store manager for Verizon for the last 2 years, then you will be labeled and perceived as a store manager in the cellular phone business.

For these reasons we must change our materials to change the perceptions people will have of us. Otherwise, our resume will sabotage us, instead of helping us.

This sample of the functional resume below is from a client who had been in the hotel and resort industry for years, only to lose her job at what she considered the peak of her career. She then accepted a much lower salary at a retail grocery chain. She was there for nearly four years when she lost that job. She was devastated to be unemployed again. She also hated working retail, along with the hours and the compensation.

This job seeker was an excellent candidate for the functional resume. In fact, the resume below changed the entire perception of her and her abilities. If she had used a chronological resume, she would have been labeled as a Human Resources/Shopping Advocate with nearly 4 years of retail store background. The revising of the resume to a functional resume, turned the perception of her to a highly accomplished Sales and Marketing professional with honed skills in business development, coupled with operations and human resource experience.

Using the Professional Profile as a guide, she crafted this resume. Six weeks later she landed her dream job as a Director of Sales within the Assisted Living industry that paid nearly doubled her salary.

NOTE: Even though this resume exceeds 2 pages, it's OK. As long as what you are offering is creating value and getting the point across, a resume 1, 2 or even in some cases, 3 pages is fine.

Example 6

SUMMARY

Diverse business background with 20+ years experience serving the hospitality and retail industries in **sales, marketing, business development, operations and human resources**.

PROFESSIONAL PROFILE

Sales

- Hospitality Director of Sales with a client base up to $5M of Association, Corporate and SMERF business.

- Was responsible for the top 10 producing accounts at three different resorts.

- Built and maintained strong business relationships with clients resulting in 70% re-booking of my overall annual group business. A sampling of clients included various NYS Teaching Associations, NJ Stat First Aid, NYS Council Knights of Columbus, NYS Sons of Italy, UJF Jewish Choral Festival, Ames Department Stores, Lucent Technologies and Sodexo.

- Increased regular guest sales as much as 30% with value added programs opposed to discount rate offers.

Marketing

- Trade Show Developer & Promoter for Bon Secours Health Systems Surgical Weight Loss Expo.

- Trade Show Developer for Hospitality Green/Pennsylvania Highlands Conservancy Green Tourism Conference dedicated to Green Tourism Branding for the Delaware River basin in New York and Pennsylvania.

- Created Innovative hospitality marketing materials to develop underserved markets and spark revenue opportunities.

- Spearheaded Internet Marketing Campaign for a resort enhancing website optimization and online reservations.

- Developed marketing strategy for a major supermarket chain to build relationships and increase sales. Through community outreach I engaged schools, senior centers, municipalities, The Maria Ferrari Hospital and various religious organizations with creative programs and events to support their needs and in turn grow loyal shoppers and revenues.

- Constructed themed resort travel packages in collaboration with area attractions for individual travelers.

- Designed a Leisure Learning Program for seniors that coupled a resort vacation with programs from the local college.

Business Development

- Built and grew a collection agency that employed 7 people and reached $1M of active accounts.
- Developed meeting planning business that reached top annual booking of $500,000.
- Grew relationships and developed programs specific to the needs for ShopRite Supermarkets with the Orange County Department of Health, Rothman Productions, and TSB Bariatric Centers.

Operations

- Hospitality Director of Convention Services for facility with 60,000 ft² of meeting space that spanned two side-by-side resorts with the capacity to serve up to 2500 guests.
- Revenue Manager for 1200 room resort.
- Reservation Manager for hospitality facilities that ranged from 400 – 1200 rooms and up to 3000 people.
- Supervised departments of 6 – 22 people.

Human Resources

- HR Manager for retail store employing 290 people as administrator of general HR functions.
- Aligned company need for developing a workforce that delivers exceptional customer service. Initiated strategies to strengthen employee engagement through heightened communications, a rewards and recognition program based on performance

and behavior and interactive seminars to build empowerment and self-confidence.

- Authored a policy and procedure manual for a 400 room resort.
- Proficient in Kronos and training applications for OSHA and HIPPA.

Employment History

- **General Manager**, Epiphany LCE Enterprises, 2009 to Present
- **HR Manager/Shopper Advocate**, ShopRite Supermarkets, Inc, 2010 to 2014
- **Senior Sales Manager and Marketing Manager**, Hudson Valley Resort and Spa, 2007 – 2009
- **Director of Sales**, Kutsher's Country Club, 2003 – 2007
- **Director of Convention Services**, Nevele Grande Resort 1997 – 2003

Professional Affiliations, Certifications and Education

- AAS Degree in Business Administration
- Certified Meeting Professional (CMP)
- Certified in Green Facility Management
- Hospitality Sales and Marketing International (HSMAI) Hudson Valley Chapter, Chapter Chair, Board of Directors

- SHRM member, Board of Directors as Meetings Chair
- Sullivan County Leadership Advanced Studies Graduate through the Chamber of Commerce
- Professional Women of Sullivan County member, Board of Director, Past President
- SCORE Sullivan County, Co-Founder, Chair, Board of Directors

Honors

- Academic Honor Society Phi Theta Kappa
- Professional Women of Sullivan County Scholarship
- Stewart's Convenience Store ESC Scholarship

Languages

- Proficient in Conversational Spanish

Example 7

SUMMARY

Diverse business background with 20+ years of experience serving the healthcare, financial, chamber of commerce and hospitality industries in sales, marketing, business development, event planning and operations. I pay close attention to the big picture and can react quickly with innovative solutions, solving complex problems, thinking critically and communicating clearly both in writing and verbally.

- 20+ years of experience in $1M to $640M organizations
- Developed strategic partnerships and alliances with community, non-profit and for profit organizations, political and investor support for healthcare, chamber, financial and casino resort project
- Event planner, organizer, fundraiser, public speaker and host for over 120+ events
- Corporate compliance leader for policies and procedures for corporations, employees and board members
- Leader of workforce training programs with State of New York (SUNY) colleges, workforce investment boards (WIB) and board of cooperative educational services (BOCES) in Hudson Valley region
- Spokesperson for projects and writer of bi-weekly newsletter

- Team building and leader of office operations including membership development, healthcare insurance, corporate compliance, fundraising, budget and board of directors
- Fiscal oversight and improvements of $100M in operating budget including federal, state and county contracts

Sales

- Developed, negotiated and won over 150 government contracts in excess of $20M
- Sold over 300+ Chamber of Commerce memberships and sponsorships; investment and insurance accounts
- Created new "750 Project" to successfully fund an entire new website and database system
- Won investments of $1.1M with two investors for casino project development

Marketing

- Develop strategy plan for re-development of new website including wireframe, newsletter, sales and news releases, search engine optimization (SEO)
- Promotion of organizations through events, social media, radio and television
- Author of news articles, periodicals and newsletters

Business Development

- Building of relationships through contact and events with prospective and existing clients resulting in hundreds of referrals, new members, investors and accounts

- Created databases with prospective and client information

Operations

- Leader of organizations policies, procedures, compliance, fundraising, budget, healthcare insurance and office operations.
- Regular meetings and communications that are clear, in writing and verbally, to confirm and profess goals of organization.

Employment History

- Nevele Resort, Casino & Spa,
  Ellenville NY   12/13 – 12/14
  Vice President, Community Relations
- New Paltz Regional Chamber
  of Commerce, New Paltz NY   01/12 – 11/13
  President
- Elant, Inc., Goshen NY   09/06 – 01/11
  Vice President, Chief Compliance
  Officer/Foundation Liaison
- Advest/Pucci Investment Group,
  Goshen NY   04/01 – 01/06
  Financial Advisor
- J. & H. Smith Light Corporation,
  New Windsor NY   01/90 – 04/01
  Co-Chief Executive Officer & Partner

Education and Training

- Marist College, Bachelor of Arts, Business Administration
- Credentialed Certified Compliance Executive (CCE)
- Licensed NYS Broker and Agent for Life, Accident and Health
- NYS Notary Public

Professional Affiliatons

- NYS Governor's Regional Advisor Committee for Health Benefit Exchange
- SUNY New Paltz School of Business board advisor and business plan judge
- Catskill Hudson Area Health Education Center board member
- Chamber of Commerce board member of two New York State organizations
- United States, Metropolitan and Hudson River golf association member

Honors/Recognitions

- Competent Toastmaster (CTM) International
- Holden Home Annual Salute to Seniors Award
- Author of best-selling business golf book ranked #1/Top Ten 2001-2010
- Certificate of Achievement for 2009-2010 Healthcare Best Compliances Forum

CHAPTER 11

THE COVER LETTER

The Key to Creating Activity

The cover letter is the 'Getting Started' portion of your marketing materials. Your cover letter's purpose is to demonstrate to the reader within 6 to 8 seconds that you are the person they need to interview as you are addressing their specific needs (as demonstrated in their *job description.)*

Targeting the needs of the employer by aligning your skills, expertise and accomplishments with their needs you will get the immediate attention of the reader. HR and recruiters love this as it simplifies their work. They don't have to decipher or hunt through a lengthy resume to determine your value and it helps them communicate who you are to decision makers.

The vast majority of cover letters are not read. I have talked to dozens of Human Resource Professionals and the vast majority of them admit to skipping the cover letter and going directly to the resume.

Why is this? Because most cover letters are written in *paragraphs* about the job seeker's interest in the position, how ideal they believe they are for the position (whether or not they really are), stating where they saw the job advertised and conclude with *see attached resume for your review.*

With the slightest glance, any recruiter or HR personnel can see this. So they rarely bother reading it. They think they already know what it says. So they pass over it and turn to the resume.

Think about it: If you received with your new digital camera a Getting Started Guide that stated *Please see attached manual to figure out how to operate your new camera*—what would you think?

The Cover Letter needs to be the 'Getting Started' guide, taken from your Professional Profile.

The resume is usually the boring, long winded manual that nobody wants to read, and when they do, they usually give it a 7 to 12 second glance.

A power packed, hard hitting cover letter will immediately increase your odds in getting interviews if you are able to address their needs.

Below is an example of a cover letter that was very effective in reaching decision makers, getting interviews and landing a great job.

Note that it references the open position and job identifier in the heading. This eliminates the usual boring paragraph describing the open position. This also demonstrates the candidate's ability to write a professional business letter and helps the reader by quickly identifying the job to which you are applying.

The first sentence then informs the reader how they align directly with the job description—going immediately to the employer's targeted needs. *These targeted needs align exactly with those from the job description.* Following this are succinct bullets of how the candidate meets those needs. In conclusion, is a brief paragraph stating attachments and the applicant's interest in meeting to discuss their needs.

Example 8

XYZ, Inc
000 Harristown Road
White Plains, NY

RE: Open Position – Senior Product Development Analyst / Job ID 65789

Dear Sir/Madam:

Based on your need for a Senior Product Development Analyst as outlined in the job description, I believe that my experience, knowledge and skills appear to be an excellent match:

- Over 25 years of experience in the insurance industry, with extensive experience in Compliance, Product Development, Underwriting, Communications and Marketing.
- Hold a CPCU designation, as well as a current New Jersey Producer's license.
- Forte is state filings, having spent the last 15 years in that discipline with 9 years of experience with the SERFF filing application.
- Filings submitted were on a countrywide, multiple line Property/Casualty basis, for both personal and commercial lines.
- Recognized for being detail oriented, congenial, easy to work with and I have a collaborative work style.

I have included a skills alignment chart and my resume for your review. I would welcome the opportunity to explore with you how I might be able to meet your needs in the state filings department.

Thank you for your consideration.

Sincerely,

The following letter also aligns with the needs of the company and job description as well. Short, concise, warm and professional, it is guaranteed to be read and the candidates skills easily understood and easily passed on.

Example 9

XXX, Inc.
NY, NY

RE: z/OS Systems Programmer

Director of Support and Services,

This interesting position, as outlined in the job description would appear to directly benefit from my 30 months z/OS experience at IBM and 7 months at NYC Transit.

My core corporate IT competencies are:

- Senior Systems Programmer Engineer.
- Specialist mainframe network, automation and problem analysis.
- Corporate IT systems remediation and compliance projects.
- Disaster Recovery Engineer.

Your consideration is appreciated. Please call, XXX-XX-XXX or email, *xyz@abc.net* to move to the next step.

Sincerely,

The cover letter is the 'Getting Started' of your marketing program. Use it effectively to address how you are the solution to their problem. Keep it brief, simple, aligned with their needs and watch your ratio of interviews increase.

CHAPTER 12

THE SKILLS ALIGNMENT MATRIX

The Skills Alignment Matrix is a table or outline that aligns your experience, expertise and skill sets with the needs of the employer. Simply lift those needs from the job description, paste them into the table and describe how you will meet that need, possess that experience, have that degree, etc.

The Skills Alignment Matrix helps the person receiving it to quickly align you with the job and get you in for a face to face interview. This powerful and useful tool can then be passed along to others without the need for the interviewer to 'wing it' to others trying to describe your skills and accomplishments.

A very effective tool in interviewing is to give your Skills Alignment Matrix to the interviewer. This will often become the point of focus, impress upon them you have done your homework, gone far above the call of duty and know your material.

Many who have used this tool claim "The skills alignment sheet is what got me the job!" Often adding "The interviewer loved it as it made their work so much easier."

The Skills Alignment Matrix is very effective as a follow-up to an interview. Sent along with a follow-up to the thank you letter, it creates an impression that will set you apart from the other candidates. It will make you memorable and prove beyond a doubt that you can meet their needs, and present yourself in a professional and dynamic way.

It is also an excellent exercise before an interview. By writing down how you align with the requirements of the job order, you will 'own' the job, probably even better than the interviewer.

Don't allow your career to be contingent on a stranger's ability to effectively communicate your value to a third party.

Skills Alignment Matrix (SAM)

Job Description	*Candidate*
- Develops and implements strategic marketing plans, sales plans and forecasts to achieve corporate objectives.	- Developed strategic marketing plans for sales, service, customer support, websites, e commerce, products, services, mergers, software, and app. Implemented sales plans to drive sales by market segment, territories, products, quotas and overachievement goals.
- Develops and manages sales/marketing operating budgets.	- Managed P & L for sales and marketing budgets to deliver growth and profitability. Managed by territory, product line, customer and overall portfolio.
- Directs sales forecasting activities and sets performance goals/metrics accordingly, holding sales representatives accountable.	- Forecasted through Salesforce.com to track stage of sales process and likelihood of closing. Measured projections of close dates, run rates and new business additions. Daily call activity tracked through phone system software. Task system in SF tracked accountability of activities and tasks to be completed

- Directs staffing, training, and performance evaluations to develop and control sales and marketing programs.	- Recruited and hired sales reps through Schools, Networking, Linked in, Recruiters, etc. Provided in house and outside resources for training goals. Monthly 1-1 with each rep to review goals, campaign results and deal strategies
- Directs market channel development activity and coordinates sales distribution by establishing sales territories, quotas, and goals.	- Developed new geographical markets in U.S. and export business. Expanded brands and new product categories to grow sales. Established territories throughout U.S. and NY Metro areas. Set up account assignments, portfolios. quotas, and goal setting.
- Meets with key clients, assisting sales representatives with maintaining relationships and negotiating and closing deals	- Met with customers and prospects to maintain accounts and develop new business relationships. Approved all deals in market.
- In conjunction with outside marketing firm, plans and oversees advertising and promotion activities.	- Worked with outside and inside marketing and IT firms to develop social media, e commerce, advertising, trade shows and website development.

- Develops and recommends product positioning and pricing strategy to produce the highest possible long-term market share.	- Created new product development process to expand line in an organized way. Pricing established based on competitive positioning and profit margin goals. Managed entire product life cycle.
- Achieves satisfactory profit/loss ratio and market share in relation to preset standards and industry and economic trends.	- VP of Sales in largest market in the country. Experience expanding market share through merger and acquisition. Successful at achieving profit goals throughout career.
- Oversees and evaluates market research and adjusts marketing strategy to meet changing market and competitive conditions.	- Conducted market research through surveys and acted on results to increase sales, customer satisfaction and operational improvements.
- Monitors competitor products, sales and marketing activities.	- Performed SWOT analysis on each competitor. Focused on areas of strength for our company against each competitor. Created knowledge management file for each rep to access.
- Establishes and maintains relationships with industry influencers and key strategic partners.	- Secured relationship with largest industry buying group. Gave presentations at trade shows. Worked with all vendors at all levels.

- Establishes and maintains a consistent corporate image throughout all product lines, promotional materials, and events.	- Consulted and implemented 2 major brand change initiatives after nationwide mergers. Created private label products and programs,
- Business Acumen. - Communication Proficiency. - Customer/Client Focus. - Leadership. - Presentation Skills. - Problem Solving/Analysis. - Results Driven. - Strategic Thinking. - Computer skills, especially CRM and ERP systems. - Experience developing B2B e-Commerce platforms.	- Ongoing consistent success in each of these areas. Have experience with Sage Sales Logix, Salesforce.com, Oracle, Clarify call center, as-400 and VAM ERP. - Planned, developed and implemented transition to ecommerce platform. 30 % of business moved through this channel. - M.B.A. Management - B.S. Marketing

PART III

POWERFUL TOOLS TO LEVERAGE YOUR JOB SEARCH

A set of powerful tools for the job search venture can lead to maximum success. Stop wondering 'what to do' and start thinking 'which tools should I use' to get results.

CHAPTER 13

APPLYING ONLINE—
THE 3-PRONG APPROACH

Applying to jobs online has become the norm on a worldwide basis. It seems it's the unwritten law—apply online, or don't apply at all!

Yet, the success rate of applying online is surprisingly low. There are many reasons for this:

- It was never received (the internet is notorious for this).
- It didn't make it through the (ATS) Applicant Tracking System (or it scored too low).
- Your resume was formatted into a system that made it illegible.
- The recruiter / HR didn't understand how well you align with the position.
- You were among the other 500 resumes they received and you were simply skipped over.

- The recruiter doesn't understand what the hiring manager is looking for, so he fails to pass you on.

- Talent Acquisition perceived you as being 'too seasoned' or 'over qualified' and was reluctant to pass you on.

- They are looking for the 'perfect' candidate (there are very few perfect candidates).

- They are only interviewing 7 people—3 internal, 2 from recruiters and 2 from referrals, so where does that leave the online submissions.

Countless times job seekers have called to confirm receipt of their resume and have been told—it hasn't been received, or that is didn't match their needs. Take a moment to think how bad this is for the job seeker and also the company. The perfect candidate is passed up because the Talent Acquisition (in-house recruiter) didn't understand that a Relationship Manager in some banks is actually a Teller. Or that an organic chemist may have all the credentials for a quality control chemist but their titles are different? Or perhaps the perfect candidate has not inserted the right percentage of industry specific buzzwords of the position to get through the Applicant Tracking System. This is a tragedy for both applicant and employer

Successfully applying online requires more than just following their directions, filling out applications and attaching a cover letter and resume. It requires the 3 Prong Approach that will greatly enhance your ability to get your materials to the hiring managers and get what you are aiming for—more interviews.

Alfred, a Supply Chain professional, unemployed for 3 months wasn't getting any results from his job search. 30+ resumes sent out had resulted in only a few phone calls from prospective employers. When we met he was extremely agitated, and angry.

"I don't get this at all! This is crazy! I have 20 years experience in the industry and I'm being treated like a piece of dog crap!"

Then I explained his problem. He was sending all his materials to *non-decision makers* who probably didn't understand the role of Supply Chain and Procurement. That his resume was probably preventing him from getting interviews due to a number of factors i.e. age, being unemployed; and furthermore, the difficulty by Talent Acquisition in understanding his 'fit' due to the nature of the job. I also asked him.

"Why, as a professional are you only going to non-decision makers? Shouldn't you be going to those that know and understand what you do?"

Then Alfred starting applying the 3 Prong Approach to every job he applied to and started watching the number of interviews soar to as high as 80% of send outs. Within another 3 months, and 6 interviews later, he landed a job at a hospital that paid him nearly as much as his previous salary. Then 6 weeks later he was contacted by another company he had sent his materials to, and they offered him substantially more, and he took it.

"My strategy was to *apply on line and follow up to a Decision Maker with my cover letter and my Professional Profile—not my resume.* I then would attempt to call the Decision Maker and usually leave a message. I started to get calls from Human Resources telling me they had received my materials from 'Upper Management' and that's why they were calling. Not once did I get a call telling me they received my materials online!"

"The 3 Prong Approach takes some work, and some courage, but once you get past that (initial stage) and start using it, it works like magic" he told the workshop after landing his new job.

So what is the 3 Prong Approach?

Prong 1: When applying online be sure they see your cover letter first (in the format as described above), preferably before your resume. On many application platforms this can be a separate attachment. Or in the case a single attachment is required, simply create a single document with the cover letter first and the resume second. Or in many cases, your cover letter, Professional Profile, Skills Alignment Matrix—then your resume at the end if you think it is necessary. (Many find they don't need the resume) Remember, if your resume is hurting you, don't use it! *We are aiming to generate phone calls* that lead to interviews, always keep that in mind.

Note: If applying online is not getting you any results, and furthermore is taking up hours of your valuable time, then simply skip Prong 1 and go directly to Prong 2. An increasing number of job seekers are finding that applying online is simply a waste of time. The question you need to ask yourself is, what is more pertinent— Sending your information to an ATS system or getting it directly to a Decision Maker?

Prong 2: Insert a printed copy of your cover letter (as is demonstrated above), along with your Professional Profile, into an envelope. Hand write the name of the recipient (a Decision Maker, i.e., a department head or even the CEO of the company), write CONFIDENTIAL under the address, put a stamp on it and send it out in the mail.

You should also send an email directly to a Decision Maker. Be sure to 'cc' the Decision Maker so that he receives the same mail twice in a row. You must also have a subject line that is going to prompt them to open it. Also be sure to copy and paste your Cover Letter and Professional Profile into the email, not send as attachment. People are reluctant to open an attachment, and you are aiming for maximum attention upon opening.

If this is for a job you've found advertised that implies no phone calls etc., you can express in the cover letter "I have applied online as instructed and I also wanted to submit directly to you out of professional courtesy." This way they know you have followed company protocol.

By sending your marketing materials directly to decision makers, you are:

- Making sure your material gets to the company and to a Decision Maker.

- Sending a powerful message to the Decision Makers that you are different, far more business oriented, and you understand the importance of reaching out to those that can make decisions.

- Demonstrating that you think vertically instead of like everyone else.

- You are hitting them 3 times (effective marketing usually requires a minimum of 5 points of exposure before a sale). Robert Clay of *Marketing Wisdom* states "It takes at least FIVE continuous follow up efforts after the initial sales contact, before a customer says "Yes".

- Increasing the odds of your material to be taken seriously. As your materials will almost inevitably be passed down to Human Resources, they will be far more motivated to reach out to you which can easily translate into an interview.

Many job seekers believe that bypassing HR you might be overstepping the line or breaking with protocol. This is a myth. The vast majority of Human Resource professionals we have contacted over the years state that they welcome getting a resume or other material from a hiring manager. Why? It makes their job easier as they don't have to browse through a pile of resumes. They can also now concentrate on this 'referral' passed down to them from a Hiring Authority. And, if it inevitably turns out to be a bad hire, they won't be the first to blame.

One Talent Acquisition professional in a workshop in was asked how she felt if she was handed materials from the Hiring Manager.

"I would act on it. It would make my life easier and I would call the person, absolutely!"

On the job seeker's end, you are suddenly the point of attention. You've been singled out and put to the top of the pile. Most importantly, as stated above, there is a high probability of being contacted by HR if your materials were handed down to them by management.

In the event you did not present a resume (and only the cover letter and Professional Profile), and they phone you asking to 'see your resume', ask them what it was that attracted their attention. Try to engage them into a dialogue, with a goal of finding out their needs. Then move the conversation along to meeting them face to to face.

"Would tomorrow or the following day at 8 or 9 in the morning be a good time to meet and drop off my resume?" Refrain from simply giving in to them and sending them your resume. Keep in mind, your materials prompted the phone call. Now turn the phone call into an interview.

Never be afraid to to schedule the interview yourself. Recruiters do it all the time. After all, it's only a business transaction, and you simply want to meet with them to determine if you would be a good fit.

Prong 3: Follow up with a phone call to confirm receipt of your materials. Preferably this is a voicemail left at 7:00 in the morning. The early time impresses them, you usually can get through any gatekeepers, and most importantly, it leaves a *warm calling card*—which makes further follow ups easier.

Example

"Good morning John, this is Jackie Evans and I am just following up on the materials I sent you last week in reference to the Director of Marketing position. Just to recap on who I am ...." Then lay out 3 or 4 great points from your professional profile.

- (I have) 15+ years in the advertising industry
- My clients have included Dial, McDonalds, and J-Crew ... and
- I have increased revenue for my clients as much as 200% annually

Then close out by saying:

"I would welcome the chance to have a dialogue about your needs, and I can be reached at xxx-xxx-xxxx repeat (slowly) xxx-xxx-xxxx. Thank you for your time and have a wonderful day!"

This 3 Prong Approach has done the following:

- Put you in contact with the company 3 times, and with a Decision Maker twice.

- It has shown you are innovative and creative in your profession.

- Your well conceived and targeted materials addressing their needs, will spark their interest.

- Following up as promised in your cover letter will warrant a nod of approval.

- Your warm professional voicemail demonstrating your value in real time (targeted at their needs) will also impress them, and see you as a human ... not a one-dimensional resume.

This technique is simple, direct, helpful to all parties and puts you in control. Those that use it report great success. Start using it when you apply to companies and watch the number of responses and interviews grow.

CHAPTER 14

THE 30-SECOND MOVIE TRAILER

Media production giants know how to get people to want more. They show us a few riveting scenes, including one of the most thrilling moments, from their newest release, and we're scrambling to get tickets for the first showings. Take your cue from them the next time you're asked that dreaded question: Tell me about yourself?

Most people want to start at the beginning of their career and move forward. This is generally best to be avoided due to the law of diminishing returns. The more you ramble on, the more the listener's interest diminishes. Not a good thing when it could mean the difference between a great job and staying unemployed.

The key to this question is engaging the listener. Tell them what you are. If you are a Creative Director, then tell them. Follow this with the names of the companies you have worked with (if the companies are going to make an impact). Then let them know the industries you have been in; all along thinking strategically how you are aligning with their needs. Then follow that up with names and numbers of interest to them.

I had a 65 year old sales professional from the garment industry in a workshop one day. When I asked her to tell us about herself, she simply said she had been in the garment industry. I then asked her what was one of her biggest deals. She replied: "I was the first person in the industry to sell fashion goods to Walmart, which actually was a $2.5 million order".

Of course with that statement, the entire perception of her changed and the rest of the attendees were forever more impressed with her; and would never forget it either.

Using your Professional Profile, start to create powerful statements that you can use in conversations and interviews—and practice speaking them until you *own* them.

Memorize your Professional Profile bullet points. Pick up the phone and send a voicemail to yourself. Practice your 30-second trailer with your friends or family members. Within a few days you will have it down, and with regular practice, you'll always be ready to give a powerful personal presentation in real time.

CHAPTER 15

EVERYBODY IS HIRING, EVEN IF THEY ARE FIRING

Everybody is hiring, even if they are firing—this is in the minds of all successful recruiters. This should be your mindset as well.

Companies are always looking for the best and the brightest talent. And real talent, even in the midst of high unemployment, *is hard to find*.

While Bank of America may be laying off 1000 employees, you can bet they are looking for another new 100 to fill in the gaps. Will they be advertising this immediately? Probably not. Yet, if you are able to get through to a hiring authority and convey to them your value and that you are real talent to be reckoned with, it's a good chance you may get an interview.

Keep in mind that many layoffs have to do with incoming managers that are bent on cleaning house. It is common practice to layoff those that don't align with the new manager's visions. This 'out with the old and in with the new' mentality, can be a perfect opportunity for open positions.

Consider every employer you ever worked for in the past. How often were people let go on the spot with no replacement in reserve? How often are companies scrambling for new hires, even when they are firing?

Don't let the media and bad news sway you. Everybody is hiring, even if they are firing. Your job is to find out the company's needs and communicate to the decision makers that you are the solution to their problems. Turn this negative situation into a positive one in your favor and market yourself even in the midst of layoffs and downsizings.

CHAPTER 16

THEY CAN'T FIND YOU AND YOU CAN'T FIND THEM

Somewhere there is a company looking for someone with your exact skill set and experience; problem is, they can't find you, and you can't find them.

When you were employed, good recruiters could easily find you. Company websites and directories, word of mouth, LinkedIn, etc. You had leverage and credibility. Co-workers and associates knew you, and you had numerous opportunities to mingle with those within your sphere of influence. You'd pick up the phone, talk to an associate, and you were soon setting up a lunch date to discuss opportunities.

Now you are sitting in a room with a computer and sending off countless resumes and feeling very alone and isolated.

You may be thinking "I've posted my resume on numerous job boards and anyone can find me. You've sent out so many resumes to so many companies, that everybody knows you. You've spoken to half a dozen recruiters and they know you as well. You are on LinkedIn and the whole world can see you."

So what is the problem? Your resume may be all over the internet, but who is looking at it? Perhaps insurance companies offering entry level sales jobs? Commission only based businesses trying to sell windows and doors? Sound familiar? You bet. Job boards are gold mines for such companies as well as anyone who can gain access to them. But are they helping you?

The other half of this equation is, you can't find them. If only a small percentage of jobs are advertised on line, due to a number of factors, i.e., advertising costs, the vastness of the web, the fact the position hadn't been through the 'internal' process, etc., how can you find those that need you and will hire you? You need to go directly to the source.

Identify those companies you want to work for—those companies that align with your skills and experience. Then start strategically marketing yourself to them. Go to their career sites and see if there are any openings. If not don't give up. Go on LinkedIn and find the head of the department you are interested in and send them a marketing letter that addresses their needs and your Professional Profile. Your goal is to get noticed, get phone calls, and be recognized as a professional that is highly proactive in your job search endeavors.

CHAPTER 17

THE EMPTY SEAT MENTALITY

Well before a job opening is posted online, it is likely that position has actually been open for a long time.

When you were working for your previous employer, you knew that John, the head supervisor, was unhappy and was secretly looking for another position. Mary in payroll was recently engaged and planning to move to New Zealand in July. Your boss was stressing out, gaining weight and was inching himself closer to a heart attack on a daily basis. This is the point—*you knew* all these people would be gone within a matter of time, sometimes within a few weeks or months.

That same scenario is being played out in every company around the world. People are holding positions that, sooner or later, for a multitude of reasons, will be vacated.

Companies are also looking for the very best talent. A happily employed VP of Quality Control and Logistics may be giving all he's got, and he's good, but there is always someone better. Perhaps it's you? The owner of a well established NY accounting firm stated to me "people upgrade their cars, their boats, their homes, so why shouldn't I upgrade my employees if a better one comes along"? Incidentally, one did come along, knocking on his door one day in person, and he let go of an accountant who had been with the firm 10 years—and hired someone with more skills and expertise. These are the realities of the marketplace.

Another scenario is successful companies are growing. That means they are looking to hire, even if they don't know it yet. Ask any good recruiter, and you'll find a large number of their open job orders are newly created positions.

If the job is an open position, you just might beat the competition of other job seekers by getting in early. Keep in mind, though, when that position does become available, employers first try to fill it internally, through contacts, word of mouth, etc. It may be weeks before the position is even published for the world to see.

If it is to be believed, according to numerous sources on the internet, that only a small percentage of jobs are publicly advertised, then where are the other jobs? (Incidentally, whether this fact is true or not, logistically it is nearly impossible to locate every possible opportunity that is published.)

To put all your efforts into applying for the few jobs you find online places you in the pool of candidates who are all competing for that same position. Once the position is posted online, you can bet applicants will be pouring in from all over the country, and even the world.

Instead of stagnating in this empty seat mentality, consider this alternative approach: Start researching companies you want to work for and start making yourself available to them. In fact, you are actually doing them a favor. You are helping them find you, you are cutting out a recruiter and saving them money, and you just may give them some good ideas to start a new venture and put you in charge. Take advantage of LinkedIn, which profiles companies and provides the names of decision makers for you to contact, and markets to them. Avoid the empty seat mentality and start going after jobs you want, instead of always waiting for jobs to come to you.

CHAPTER 18

THE SOONER YOU START, THE BETTER

A common complaint we hear from those who embrace the methodology in this book is "I wish I had heard about this when I first started my search!" Actually it should be—"*Before* I started my search."

The professional mind set, the methodology and the tools of this book will get you started on the right track from the beginning. Once you launch your search, like any business venture, you will want to come out fully prepared and ready to take on the business world.

Why is starting early so important? First impressions, timing and the right mindset are crucial to success.

Friday morning at 9:30 a.m. Jim was let go. After 22 years at the same bank with consistent stellar recognition, he was told his 'performance reviews' were not satisfactory. At 9:40 a.m. he was sitting in his car in a state of shock and denial. Driving home, he began to visibly shake with rage, "How could they have done this to me?"

Now Jim sits at his laptop, scans the internet for samples of resumes and rushes to construct a resume. He's distracted, though. He's still enraged; emotions rule. He keeps seeing Lucy, the Manager of HR sitting at her desk coldly informing him of his poor reviews. His mind is already racing into the future; he's trying to explain at his first interview why he left his last job after 22 years. He's wondering how he's going to face his golfing buddies tomorrow morning.

He goes to a job website and sees a position for a Branch Manager 70 miles away at a bank he never liked. "Well beggars can't be choosers" he assures himself as he attaches his newly crafted resume to the application and shoots it off. Little does he consider, he also just allowed this 'pieced together' resume to be posted on the internet so the whole world can see. He sits back and feels a little better.

He then starts hitting every bank and financial institution he can. Sending his resume and and cover letter to every bank that has an opening. He's feeling a little better as he's convinced himself that he's doing exactly what he should be doing.

Then the phone rings, and it's a insurance company that would like to interview him. He feels uplifted. He then finds himself traveling 50 miles to see a recruiter for 10 minutes, standing in line at the labor department, and waiting for replies from the jobs he really wants—but they just don't seem to be materializing.

Three months later Jim is still unemployed and things aren't looking so good. His anger has has transformed into a mixture of anxiety, depression and hopelessness. He's starting to look at jobs he'd never considered before and he's way over qualified.

What has happened?

- Jim has launched a new business venture he is totally unfamiliar with and totally unprepared for—while in a highly emotional and anxiety ridden state of mind.

- He has marketed himself to the entire business world with materials he is not remotely familiar with and were hastily thrown together.

- By applying to every bank he can, he is now in all their candidate databases. This has just deterred most good recruiters who might want to work with him. Why? If he's in their client databases, the recruiter won't get paid.

- By posting himself online, he has also given his resume to countless unscrupulous recruiters who have sent him off to as many companies as possible to secure their position in the 'race to the database'.

- Without being fully prepared with a great presentation, impressive marketing tools that address an employer's needs and the Professional Job Seekers acumen to follow-up and contact decision makers, he is throwing his ability to make a great presentation out the window, and ending up in the rejection bin.

- He is wasting precious time that is robbing him of both potential income, eroding his professionalism, and causing stress the longer he stays unemployed; and as the days turn into months, he is creating perceptions to employers that he is unemployable.

- When Jim finally does get a call and even potential interview from a worthy employer, he is not properly prepared for the interview, and finds himself still unemployed—and just as bad, he blew a great to opportunity that could have put him back to a work.

These are just a few examples of what happens when one starts the job search unprepared and without a strategic plan. Don't let it be you. Those who started early in the process, even while still employed, seamlessly transitioned over to a better job faster and with far more leverage. The sooner you start—the better.

CHAPTER 19

TAKING CONTROL OF PERCEPTIONS

How people perceive us and our own perceptions of the world can play a dramatic role in the job search. If it is true that nearly 100% of reality is perceptions, then *controlling* perceptions is the key to opening doors for us— or potentially keeping them closed.

Let's explore some common perceptions that job seekers have:

1. A resume is always required.
2. Dates must be included on your materials.
3. You must always go through Human Resources first.
4. A CEO will be annoyed if you contact them.
5. When asked what you are you looking to make, you must give a figure.
6. 'No phone calls' means you cannot call them.
7. You're over 50 so getting a job is extremely hard.
8. The job is filled so you've lost the chance to work for that company.

9. It's not what you know, it's who you know.
10. Since you don't have all the necessary skills for the job, don't bother applying.

Every one of these perceptions can be countered and turned around to a job seeker's advantage. Yet these same perceptions (and there are many more) are what is keeping so many people unemployed.

If your chronological resume is sabotaging your efforts to get an interview because you've been out of work too long, perhaps it's time to focus the attention of those reading it to your skills and accomplishments (and away from dates) by using a functional resume, or even a Professional Profile with no dates.

If Human Resources are not perceiving you to be a great fit because the nature of the job is too complex for them to understand, perhaps you need to bypass Human Resources and get straight to a Decision Maker.

By realizing that the interview process begins with the materials you send in, and what you send in is how you will be perceived, using tools such as the Professional Profile and Skill Alignment Matrix can get you moved to the top of the pack as you have impressed those in the screening process how talented you are for the job.

No matter where you are in the job search, be aware that perceptions, and how you are perceived play a paramount role. By realizing this, you can use it to your advantage, and overcome obstacles that would otherwise sabotage your efforts.

CHAPTER 20

DEALING WITH AGE DISCRIMINATION STRATEGICALLY

One of the most common concerns among job seekers is age discrimination. Yet at the time of this writing, during the span of 2 months, 10 members of The Job Club (See overturn) secured permanent employment at companies they wanted to work for—at compensation levels higher than most had been making at their previous jobs.

How did they tackle the issue of age discrimination? They focused on an employer's needs. They awed the employers with their strengths, expertise, and experience. *They controlled perceptions of age, gaps of unemployment, lengths of period they hadn't done something pertinent to the job, location, etc., with carefully crafted marketing tools that were able to control bad perceptions by eliminating them and focusing on facts and expertise the employer would find favorable.*

For example, by using pertinent points (those that focus on the needs of the employer) taken directly from the Professional Profile, you can showcase your strengths without alluding to dates, which can eliminate you from the race almost immediately.

Undoubtedly, age is a factor, as is being unemployed, being fired, and any and all other factors that may be perceived negatively.

The key here is to control the perception of these factors, so by the time they do surface, they just don't matter, they are irrelevant to the employer. Remember that the job search is all about meeting the employer's needs. Bring out the strengths that put you in a favorable light and leave out those factors that may bring along negative perceptions. The influence of first impressions cannot be overemphasized.

Oct & Nov 2015

Name	Age	Profession	Time out	Compensation
Bill	65	Supply Chain	13 months	$100k
Hank	67	Sales	6 months	$65k
Karen	65	Garment Industry	6 months	$80k
Jessica	50	Marketing	5 months	$65k
Raquel	51	IT	5 months	$103k
Bob	67	IT	5 months	$90k
Alfred	63	Supply Chain	6 months	$95k
Bill	54	Retail	1 year	$45k
Fritz	73	Project Man	12 months	$90k
Dan	51	Sales	7 months	$135k

CHAPTER 21

IT'S A PROCESS—
SKIP A STEP AND BLOW AN
OPPORTUNITY

The job search is very much like any process that requires a number of carefully orchestrated steps to reach a successful conclusion. As circumstances warrant, the process may change, yet your chances of success greatly increase as you follow the pattern of steps laid down in this book, as you navigate the maze of a successful job search.

As an example, selling a home, you find a good agent by doing research and getting referrals and recommendations. Your agent comes up with a listing price by performing a comparative market analysis, not by just winging it. You prepare the home for sale by fixing it up and making repairs. You confirm and address all potential property easements and liens. etc. The completion of all these steps and many more is crucial even before putting the house on the market. Yet if you skip a step, say assume a termite inspection has been performed only to end up at the closing table to find the loan contingent on it, you could lose the sale.

The job search is the same. Your first order of business is understanding why the job search is so hard and reclaiming your professional mindset. Creating jaw dropping marketing materials is another indispensable step in the process. Then there are the tools to leverage your search, help you traverse HR, speak with decision makers, and make every word and minute count. Then there is the interview process that puts *you* in control, finds out *their* needs, and gets you offers. There are the steps to get the right compensation package, the right deal for you, and the list goes on. Yet, if you skip a crucial step such as not first talking to your references and coaching them on what they say about you when called by an employer, can turn a potential offer into another rejection.

The job search is a process, and there are certain steps that just cannot be ignored or bypassed. Keep the process in mind. Dot your i's and cross your t's. Start putting yourself in a professional state of mind that methodically moves you forward. Track your progress and watch yourself start to be more successful and confident in your job search.

CHAPTER 22

TIME MANAGEMENT FOR THE UNEMPLOYED

"I had *more* time when I was employed, than I do now unemployed!" Sound familiar?

Managing your time effectively while unemployed is a daunting but vital challenge for nearly all job seekers. For the first few weeks you take it easy planning to hit it hard after your recover from the loss. Or you hit it hard immediately, and in a few weeks you are burnt out, frustrated and depressed.

A laid off CEO of a major supplier of LED lights to the military walked into his first day of The Job Club and exclaimed "This is the hardest, most boring, most humiliating and most depressing work I have ever done in my entire life! I hate it ... working at a real job is a piece cake compared to this...and I don't have any time, any more either ... it's fix the sink, do the dishes, get the groceries!"

When asked how he was managing his time he replied "Whenever I can. When I have time to send out a few resumes I will. Maybe an hour here, 45 minutes there..."

This former CEO had been out of work for 13 months. Within 2 months of joining The Job Club and creating a working model for managing his time effectively, he was offered 2 jobs. His misery was now over and he was now managing his time effectively as well as his new lifestyle in being gainfully employed.

The first step in managing your time is to commit to a set schedule and sticking to it religiously. If you have a family, sit down with them and work on this together. This is imperative. Everyone must be on board with your job search, this major endeavor. It is imperative that, if you are to get back to work as soon as possible, you have quality time to focus on the job search and it is paramount that your time must be respected. During this agreed upon time, nothing is to disturb you. No trips to the market. No washing of dishes. No household errands. This is strictly work time, a day at work. Find a place to work, make sure it's a quiet work environment and stick to it.

Although everyone is different, we suggest that your job search take into account a number of factors:

- **Most productive time**—in most cases this is in the mornings. We suggest working straight through from say 7:00 a.m. to 11:00 a.m. This time will be the 'crucial time' when you are at your sharpest. Time to make phone calls, follow ups, write cover letters, hone your marketing materials, apply to jobs, reach out to decision makers, etc. This is NOT the time to scan job boards, follow up on trivial emails or read the latest gossip and news about celebrities or any other distractions. Do not squander this precious asset—your most productive time in the morning. In fact we suggest not even checking your emails until perhaps 10:00 a.m. Why? If it is important, like a potential job interview, they will call you. Emergencies are not sent via email. So you should not be in a reactive state of mind that takes up precious time. Neither should you be scanning job boards at this time. There are better times for this.

- **Break time** - at 11:00 a.m. go for a walk or exercise. Chill out and feel good that you had a productive morning. Then do your household chores that need to be done.

- **Job boards and research** - from 1:00 p.m. to 3:00 p.m. This is the time to grab a cup of coffee and start researching jobs online. Don't spend more than an hour or so at this a day. It has a tendency to burn you out and frustrate you as you pore over job descriptions that seem endless and redundant. If you identify jobs that look promising, document them and move on. When you have found perhaps 3 or 4 real potentials, stop and do research on the companies. Study their website. If the job is there on their site, then apply from there. Find out who are the decision makers. Look for directories. Google news about the company. Become a detective and make notes of all important information. This is key for the interview as well as for other interviews. Knowledge is king.

- **The evening watch** - this is the time after all has been done with the family and/or significant other. When the house is quiet and it's time to relax. In fact it can be done with your laptop sitting in front of the TV. Ideally this time is from 8:00 p.m. to 10:00 p.m. This time should be spent going on LinkedIn and researching the decision makers you need to connect with. Researching companies that YOU want to work for and don't necessarily have open positions posted. Your goal is to find 1 or 2 companies a night that have positions that align with your skills. Keep in mind, if XYZ company is in need of a person with your talents, then companies within the same industry segment probably do as well. DO NOT be concerned if they have no open positions. Just do the research and find out who are the decision makers. Last of all, before ending the day, make a list of what tasks you must do tomorrow. People you must contact, etc. This is extremely important. When you sit down at 7:00 a.m. the next day, you want to hit the ground running. Showered, casually dressed, a simple breakfast, a cup of your favorite drink, and a list of things to do, with a clear agenda for the day.

- **The weekend** - take a break. Don't even think of the job search. Let your mind and body relax and prepare for the next week. Monday morning will come around fast enough, so enjoy your life. Don't stress. Remember you have begun a process that is more productive, less stressful and is going to get you back to work. Relax, follow the process, and manage your time effectively.

CHAPTER 23

STAYING MOTIVATED

"What do you do when you've lost your oomph and drive?" was a question asked by a recent Job Club attendee. When the other ten attendees were asked if this was a problem, all of them quickly shot up their hands.

Needless to say, staying motivated, focused, and energized during the job search, especially when it comes to searching for jobs online, filling out applications, revising resumes and cover letters, etc., is crucial to both success and you own sanity.

Through numerous discussions with thousands of job seekers, the following are some key points to keep in mind to keep you sharp and motivated throughout your search.

- Commit to Time management. Knowing the amount of time you have and knowing how you are going to spend it, precious 'blocks of time' you've established to conduct a 'quality' job search, will translate into a sense of 'being employed' in a job search. It will allow time for sending out quality materials to employers, and instill a sense of accomplishment.

- Be disciplined and keep a list of things to do - Being disciplined can be a job in itself. By making a list of things to do at the end of each day, you will be able to start off quickly and with a definite goal when you resume the next day. Then as you check off your 'to do' list, you will feel a great sense of accomplishment.

- Be proactive in your job search - Get creative, think strategically, and start reaching out to Decision Makers and others that can help you. Start applying to companies *you* want to work for. You will be amazed how this process will start to create momentum, generate far more phone calls and increase direct contact with Decision Makers that will start to turn your job search into a thriving business venture.

- Go to events where you can meet people. Think of these as business meetings. You are in the business of Public Relations, so now is the time to start reaching out. Look for seminars and groups that meet that represent your profession. Become a known entity in your field and start making connections.

- Stay active on LinkedIn. Start discussions and join groups. Take advantage of the opportunity to write a blog on your profession. Keep abreast of changes in your field. Remember you *will* be back to being gainfully employed, it's only a matter of time—so use it to your advantage. Get active, get going and watch your motivation soar.

- Create new boxes - There is nothing more exciting when someone comes up with a new and creative way of doing something in the job search. Keep in mind, the traditional job search—the post and pray methodology—has been around for a long time. We have created new and highly effective tools that have worked for thousands of job seekers, yet, we have barely skimmed the surface. Create new ways of doing things. This is the time like never before to be innovative and use your business acumen to propel you forward.

- Join a Job Club and create your own 'Inner Cabinet'. Get together with other Job Seekers. If you don't have a Job Club to attend, start one. Have it first thing Monday morning—it can be a great start to a week. Find out what others are doing in their search and share your ideas. The power and energy infused into the members of a great Job Club can keep you going for days. Think of this as your 'Inner Cabinet'. Those that know the pain and frustration you are going through, and who are there for help, and to help.

- Study and research peripheral materials - Don't get bogged down, confused and potentially depressed by sticking to reading and researching job related materials. Start reading materials that can help you in the job search, but are from another discipline. Books on marketing, sales, human relationships, biographies of those that have struggled, philosophy, religion, books that deal with both the mind and body, etc. The list is endless. The goal is to refresh the mind, and to allow other disciplines to give you ideas and motivation to align with your job search, to further progress you forward.

- Get away from it all - Take some time away from the job search for 3 or 4 days. (Anytime more and you start getting rusty in this new business venture). Clearing your mind temporarily can do wonders for rejuvenating yourself—and don't feel guilty about taking this time off, consider it part of the process.

- Take a part time job you hate - This advice comes from clients who took jobs they despised, only to further motivate them to work harder on the job search. One job seeker, a certified tax accountant who had been out of work for 5 months, took an evening job as a stocker in a retail store. He hated every minute of it, yet stuck to it as he felt it motivated him to try even harder. He eventually landed a great job and never regrets the time he spent as a stocker as it gave him greater appreciation of his profession.

- Create a vision board - Put up a whiteboard on your wall and display your goals and visions. Seeing this everyday is a great motivator as it screams your affirmations to you every time you look up.

- Get your friends and acquaintances to network for you - Tell everyone you know you are looking for opportunities. This is not the time to be shy and 'too proud' to reach out. Everyone knows making contacts and 'networking' is a huge part of the job search process. Send them your Professional Profile so they will have a clear picture of who you are and what you have to offer. Think marketing and public relations at all times.

Staying motivated is crucial to being successful. Do what it takes to keep you on track. The biggest danger is falling into complacency and becoming despondent. Don't allow it to happen to you.

CHAPTER 24

JOB BOARDS—
THE GOOD AND THE BAD

The Good

Job boards are great places to find out what is happening out in the 'real world'. They can offer a wealth of information. What positions are available? Who is hiring? Where are the jobs? What are the salary ranges? Who offers great packages?

Job descriptions will give you details into jobs that you may never have considered. Perhaps that accounting job you had, coupled with your passion for drumming up members for your church can be translated into a fund raiser for a not for profit. Or your Six Sigma and 20 years in the manufacturing arena will be perfect for heading up your local Chambers of Commerce.

Like a person's social media site, job boards can give you lots of subtle information to arm you. If the position has been up for months, is that a red flag? If they fail to mention compensation or benefits, why are they keeping this a secret?

Is the company name advertised? If it is, then you know it's posted by an internal recruiter and you have to apply accordingly. If the company name is not divulged, you'll probably be dealing with a 3rd party recruiter, now it's a different game.

Some will lead to a company website that has a directory. Who is the Department Head you can contact? Who can you find on LinkedIn that you may have a relationship with?

Think of it as an inside glimpse into a company, a window into an industry that otherwise may be very hard to acquire much more than a basic understanding.

When I started out in the recruiting industry, I knew very little about banking. So I studied job postings on websites and soon I was able to talk the talk that opened doors to the industry. It's not difficult, it's just learning about an industry and the industry jargon. In fact you may find your previous position aligns very well with a position you never even considered. A Human Resources Generalist for an accounting firm may easily transition into a bank as a Branch Manager in training, if she does some research on the industry, and can demonstrate how her skills and accomplishments align with the company.

The Bad

Job boards are in the business of making money off your unemployment. The longer you stay unemployed, the more money they make. With every click, they make money. With every day your frustration increases, you are one step closer to buying their products. They are not your best friend.

Let's look at what jobs boards are not. Job boards are not all that they proclaim.

The common theme all these job boards promise, if you view them, if you submit your resume and apply to the jobs, you will get interviews and get great jobs. "Amazing Results", "Build a Better Career", "Find Your Calling", "Gets You a New Job Quicker." Yet week after week, month after month, even year after year, a large portion of job seekers who only rely exclusively on job boards and only apply online have a dismal rate of success.

It's easy to fall into a pattern of checking for jobs online and assuming it is the most productive method of finding a job. When nothing appears that aligns with your expertise, you assume there is nothing 'out there'. This is dangerous and can lead to inertia and lost momentum, as well as a longer job search.

Use job boards but don't let them become the end all in your job search. Too many job seekers see them as the golden key to success, relying on them far too much. Yes, they're are an indispensable tool—but they are only one of many.

Use job boards as a great resource and research tool, and for what they are - don't make them the all inclusive tool for your search they proclaim to be. They do not need the job—you do.

How these sites can sabotage your job search very quickly

When applying to a job online, make sure you are in control of where your resume is being sent. Nearly all commercial job boards are in the 'information' business. They want your resume so they can add it to their resume database and post this to an *exclusive* site that can only be viewed by recruiters and companies. "So what's wrong with that?"

To be able to access that exclusive site costs thousands of dollars. At a time when companies are squeezing the bottom line for every dime, does Human Resources want to pay for this? Do recruiting firms want to pay for this? Of course, some do, and you can pretty much guess who they are, the same firms advertising on the site.

Tip: When applying online, always be sure to uncheck (depends on the site) the default box that allows your resume to be posted for the world to see. Make sure it only goes to the company to which you are applying. There are a number of reasons for this.

Think of a house that has gone up in the neighborhood for sale. For the first few weeks there is a lot of attention. Then as weeks turn into months, interest in the property falls. The same occurs with your resume. The longer it is on a site, the more it is seen again and again, and soon people start to question it. This is a good example of how your resume can start to sabotage your search. It's being overlooked simply because it has been seen too many times for too long.

Note: Industry specific job sites are generally a safer place to allow your resume to be posted, yet there are still repercussions to consider. Who is looking at it? Is it how you really want to be marketed or perceived? Of course the real proof is in the results—are you getting calls from real potential employers and getting interviews?

If you are using a recruiter, we caution against putting your resume out there for all to see. Good recruiters usually don't spend a lot of time scanning job boards for resumes, and are often reluctant to work with someone who has their resume online. This is because internal recruiters at companies will scan job boards and download literally thousands of resumes to put in their database. Then when the recruiter brings a great candidate to their attention they are told "Sorry she's already in our database".

If there are any phrases the recruiter dreads hearing, this one generally tops the list. It makes for one unhappy recruiter when they realize they've wasted their time on you. Furthermore, it's embarrassing for them as it makes them look like they don't know their candidate and did a poor job screening them...which is just as bad.

A good recruiter will ask you where you have been submitted, if you are working with another recruiter or where you have submitted yourself personally. (If they don't ask you this question, they probably are new at the profession.)

This is why it's essential that you are always in control of your job search and keep track of all your send-outs, company contacts, who has your resume, etc. There is nothing like getting a call from a company you applied to 6 weeks ago, yet you can't even recall the position or the name of the company.

In conclusion, keep the job boards in perspective. They are great in what they offer, but they are *not* the final solution to the unemployed job seeker, and in fact, if not used within the methodology laid out in this book, they can lead to a very frustrated search that ends up with the same percentage of success across the board. 100 resumes sent out out with a 3 – 5% success rate of many rejection notices, a few phone calls and perhaps 1 or 2 face to face interviews.

CHAPTER 25

CAN'T GET A JOB?
IT MUST BE YOUR RESUME

This is probably one of the most common myths that plague the job seeker. They hear it from family, friends and the media. You spend countless hours perfecting it, only to find it still isn't getting you interviews. Your friends, family, and the job counselor at the local labor department who critiques it still doesn't like it. So you continue to edit it, somehow hoping you will create the 'Holy Grail' of resumes to open those doors to an interview.

Then along comes the professional resume writers to rescue you and save you from your wretched self created resume. They are the professionals you are thinking. "They know what they are doing!" "They'll get it right"! From the many online sites who claim about the thousands they have created with great results, you can't go wrong.

So you respond and pay hundreds of dollars for a resume created on a 'cookie cutter' template. The resume screams 'professionally created'. This, in fact, can turn off many recruiters and HR. "If they are so good, why do they need to have their own resume created for them?" "Does he really know what's written in this thing"?

Most professionally written resumes are full of paragraphs and hyperbole that try to impress. They are created by 'professionals' that have spent an hour or two with you. They are written with a lot of flowery fluff verbiage that sounds amazing. The resume writer doing his best to describe you, even though they don't even know you in the slightest.

Unfortunately, they are rarely the answer to your job search. In the end, they usually only impress you, and can actually backfire, sabotaging your efforts, turning off those that you truly need to impress—those who can potentially hire you.

A resume is a living breathing document. It needs to be crafted to meet an employer's needs and to get through Applicant Tracking Systems. It needs to be 'user friendly' so you can easily edit it. There is nothing more frustrating to the job seeker than having to spend time redoing their resume to every job applied to.

One professionally created resume will not cover all these bases. As few jobs are exact, this strategy is costly in both money and time. Even if you are able to edit it, they are often formatted in such a way that the slightest change turns into a two-hour ordeal of frustration.

Let's also recall what we previously discussed. *The resume, no matter how well-written, is a marketing tool that asks an employer: Guess what I can do for you? Guess how I can meet your needs?* Always keep in mind, the resume in itself, is NOT the most effective way of marketing yourself to an employer.

To put all your efforts into the resume—to assume the traditional stance of allowing the resume to be your primary tool for marketing yourself, can actually continue to keep you unemployed. By its very nature of exposing dates, unidentifiable job titles, and lengthy descriptions that have nothing to do with their needs and are too challenging to read, the resume can be giving off perceptions you cannot control.

As discussed earlier, there are far more powerful, more effective tools in getting you noticed, and getting you to the Decision Makers for an interview. So avoid the mistake of most job seekers, believing the resume is the only way to successfully get you interviews and get you hired.

Can't get a job? It must be your resume. Wrong. Resumes are not the end all for the job seeker. They are often not the most effective, and in many cases can be the *least* effective way of marketing yourself. Especially those resumes that scream 'Professionally Created' and yet are very poor at demonstrating who you really are and what you have to offer.

Start creating your *own* resume from the simple model laid out in this book. Use the tools we have provided, and start watching your efforts paid off by more interviews and better offers.

CHAPTER 26

TARGET COMPANIES YOU WANT TO WORK FOR

Imagine if you could land your dream job at the company you wanted to work. Sound crazy? Actually it's a very real possibility and now is the time (and you may finally have the time) to actually start the process of doing it.

For years you may have been (or still are) at a company that was 'bearable'. You accepted it and you felt fortunate to have it. You gradually advanced up the ladder and received your annual 3% raise a year (if you were lucky). But somewhere in the back of your mind you knew there was always something better out there. The problem was - you were too busy to look for it, or too intimidated by the process, or perhaps even too afraid to make a move.

Well, sometimes things happen in life that appear as a curse, only to turn out to be a blessing. A large percentage of the people we work with who find themselves out of work, ultimately find jobs that offer not only better compensation and culture, but turn out to be the dream job they always wanted.

How does this happen? A number of factors can contribute to this. The primary one is taking a highly proactive approach to the job search and following the process as outlined below.

The first step is to start researching the companies you want to work for and find out as much as you can about them. Don't worry about openings, just start researching them. Where are their offices and branches? Is the location realistic? What is their mission statement? Do their products and services align with your skill sets? What makes them so attractive? Research news about the company. Are they expanding? Opening up new locations? Offering new products? How are their shares doing? Google them and read the latest articles, blogs, feedback from current and former employees. Dig up anything and everything you can to learn about the company.

Next start trying to find decision makers in the company. Go to LinkedIn and check your connections. Is there someone you're linked with, linked to someone, who knows someone affiliated with the company? Keep researching and keep making notes on who is who in the company. Many company websites have directories of personnel you can reach out to. Many news articles will mention the Director of this, or the VP of that department.

Once you have found someone who is able to make decisions in the company, it's now time to start marketing yourself to them. It is important you focus your efforts on those areas in the company that need your services. The more you target your area of expertise, the closer you get to speaking with those who will be able to understand your value.

Next start sending out a finely crafted 'marketing' (see below) cover letter along with your Professional Profile.

In the cover letter, state you would welcome the opportunity to have a dialogue with them about their needs and potential opportunities in their industry. If you were able to uncover a contact number in your search, end your letter with:

"I will be following up with a call to confirm receipt of these materials and to touch base".

This can also be done via email if you are able to secure their personal email. An important key here is having an attractive subject line that gets them to open it. This can be very effective for those higher up in the food chain (CEO's, COO's, CFO's etc.,) especially on weekends and during holidays. Why weekends and holidays? This is because a vast majority of leaders at this level are highly motivated professionals with business never far from their minds. They have their smart phones, and are alert to incoming emails at all times.

Tanya, a Director of Human Resources who was let go from a major firm after a number of years, swears this was the key to her success in landing her dream job. As it was impossible to go through Human Resources given her status (they already had a Director of Human Resources), her only choice was to contact upper management and prove to them she was better than what they currently had. She was astounded how fast such people would respond on holidays and weekends. She claimed "Those that run the company are bored stiff at home and just want to get back to work. This gives them a chance to get away from it all and back to where they feel most comfortable, working." As a result she was able to secure 2 face-to-face interviews with 2 different companies and ultimately receive an offer from both of them.

Once you have mailed out your cover letter and professional profile, your next step is following up with a call a few days later.

Whether it's a voicemail or a decision maker picks up the phone, with your Professional Profile at your side, and the other tools you have access to in this book, you will be able to talk to them as a professional to another professional. Always keep in mind, you are there to help them. If you are in possession of the consultant's frame of mind, it will naturally keep you focused on their needs.

Your focus at this time is to have a dialogue, to give them enough information about yourself to pique their interest, with your primary goal of setting up a meeting to talk with them. Having dialogues leads to interviews. Interviews lead to offers.

This is not the time ask about employment opportunities. Watch this. There is a subtle yet big difference here. Asking about employment opportunities can lead to the perception of you being just another unemployed job seeker. By asking such a closed ended question can lead to a "no" and easily give them a chance to end the conversation before you even get going.

The following is one example directed at setting up a meeting, not asking about opportunities:

Job seeker: Good morning Bob.

CEO: Good morning. And who am I talking to?

Job seeker: Bob, My name is _____, and I've been a Manager of Training and Development with 15 years experience in the business. I have been with Canon and Xerox, and have been recognized as a leading expert within my industry. I also sent you some materials last week introducing myself.

Bob, I have been interested in your company for a number of years, and am intrigued by the tremendous growth, the assertive nature of your leadership, and the future that lies ahead for you in both Asia and Europe, where I see in the news you are setting up offices.

Given my expertise and background in training and development, I'd welcome the opportunity to meet with you. Perhaps there could be some alignment that could benefit us both. (Pause) How does next Tuesday at 8:30 a.m. work for you?

This type of dialogue is far more likely to get you a face to face meeting, than phone and asking about an opportunity. Create your own scripts, fit them to your career and style, and start using your professional acumen to set up meetings.

This process, like any other, will require diligence and dedication. Keep track of your progress, contacts, build your pipeline, document your work search activities. Keep in mind, like any business endeavor it is a numbers game. The more dialogues you have, the better your odds of getting in for an interview. The more interviews the closer you get to the job that is meant for you.

So start targeting companies you want to work for, send out your materials, contact them, and set up meetings. Think of yourself as a business, as a consultant. Blaze ahead and you may be pleasantly surprised when you find yourself in the CEO's office of the firm you've admired for years—all due to some simple and proactive marketing of yourself!

CHAPTER 27

THE MARKETING LETTER THAT MARKETS YOU

The marketing letter is very similar to the cover letter in that it is designed to create an immediate impact. The reader must be able to size you up and see your value, key skills and accomplishments within a matter of seconds. Less is more in most cases. The objective is to make the phone ring. Get you noticed. Make you memorable. Make it possible for the reader to easily be able to communicate who you are and what you have to offer to a third party in powerful, meaningful soundbites.

As you likely do not have a job description as a template to precisely show how you meet their needs, the marketing letter must be a glowing showpiece that demonstrates your skills and accomplishments that align with *their* company; and the specific needs that are generic to the position you are targeting.

This is where your Professional Profile comes in. Simply copy and paste those key skills and accomplishments into the body of the letter. With an interest capturing introduction and a conclusion that wraps up with your contact information, this essentially completes the marketing letter. If you feel it warrants it, you can attach your full professional profile as well to further showcase of who you are and what you have to offer.

Below are 2 examples of Marketing Cover letters that have generated results:

Example 10

Dear Dr. _____,

Are you looking for a top notch director of marketing? A seasoned professional ready to join your team who can create a brand that positions your institution as the institution across its service area? My name is _____ and I am ready to take on the challenges, armed with enthusiasm and unparalleled experience. In addition to the attached resume, please consider the following expertise I can bring to your community college.

Public relations and marketing – Created new brand identity campaigns, including both traditional and digital strategies – one campaign successfully increased enrollment by 16% at a community college and produced its first national marketing award

Social/digital media – includes the redesign of three websites; creation and launch of "Where is Knight the Panther?" Facebook campaign – increased page "Likes" by 36% in one year; production of animated United Way campaign video for YouTube; and a LinkedIn page for community college alumni (500+ connections in one year)

Budget and Planning – currently responsible for $300,000+ budget (expenses and revenues); have created/executed marketing plans for several institutions of higher education, soliciting input from and providing guidance to campus community

Proofreading and Editing – two of my strongest skills. I can spot a typo in less than 5 seconds.

Collaboration – work directly with student services providing scholarships, Foundation Board to fundraise, faculty to promote programs to attract and retain students, and campus Diversity Committee to promote this college initiative. I know my campus!

Dr. _____, I would welcome the opportunity to further discuss my credentials with you. To arrange an interview at your earliest convenience, I can be reached at my cell number, (xxx) xxx-xxxx.

Thank you for your consideration. I look forward to meeting you and to becoming the new director of marketing for _____ Community College.

Best regards,
Name

Example 11

RE: Employment Opportunities

Dear Mr. xxxxxxxxx:

Upon completion of a 20+ year sales career (primarily in Manhattan), I am looking to reposition myself in the Mid-Hudson Valley and seek an opportunity which would take advantage of my skill set. Recent research has led me to explore the healthcare industry.

As an All-American Athlete, Diving Coach at West Point, and many years of achievement in the sales and support of document hardware/software solutions; I am programmed for success.

I offer the following background:

- Extensive experience selling and supporting a wide range of hardware/software solutions and professional services.
- Ability to articulate technical solutions to non-technical clientele.
- Broad experience supporting sales teams with consultative solutions.
- Excellent presentation and communication skills.

Healthcare industry experience:

Medical Document Systems - *Worked on a team which provided production print, digital multifunction & document* *distribution/management software at* **St. Barnabas Hospital in** *the Bronx.*

Chartlogic - *Marketed/sold voice recognition medical charting software - comprehensive training on structure of medical compensation (ie: the Medicare coding models), detailed understanding of medical records and the value of EMR/ EHR & Practice Management Software.*

Managed Print Services - *Performed comprehensive data collection walkthrough, cost analysis, and ROI for Managed Print Services offerings. Worked closely with Supply Chain Directors of* **Nassau University Medical School** *(Long Island) and* **Richmond University Medical Center** *(Staten Island) learning the information/workflow processes of virtually all departments in the organizations.*

Biomedical Transport - *Served virtually all major healthcare organizations in Manhattan with Bio-medical Transport offerings. Thorough understanding of chain of custody.*

MBA in Finance.

I welcome the opportunity to begin a discussion regarding potential opportunities. Thank you for your consideration.

Sincerely,

CHAPTER 28

MARKETING LIKE A HEADHUNTER AND SOME INSIGHT ABOUT THE INDUSTRY

Those in the recruiting business spend a considerable amount of time marketing to prospective clients in order to get new job orders. Recruiters know that clients come and go, and the need to fill their pipeline with good clients is essential in staying in business. A good recruiter will manage his time by contacting at least 25 to 100 new companies a week to market an *MPC (Most Placeable Candidate) to them.

How do they find new clients? They pick up the phone and cold call companies and present MPCs to prospective clients. *They do not ask if there is a need for their services.* They present a great candidate that excites, intrigues and fulfills the needs of the listener.

I had hired Olivia to recruit for my company. With 18 years in banking, I perceived that she would excel at recruiting bankers and more specifically I was confident she could get the company new banking clients given her knowledge of banking. I told her that a particular bank had been looking for commercial lenders and I asked her to contact the bank and market an outstanding commercial lender to whom I had been introduced.

After 2 weeks I asked her how the assignment was progressing. Olivia informed me that she had called Human Resources at the company twice, and tried to submit the commercial lender. Both times they had told her to "call us back in a week as their pipeline was filled with good candidates and we are good for now".

Think about this for a moment. The Human Resources department figured they already had enough 'good' candidates, so there was no need to see another one. Yet, what if our candidate was not only a good candidate but spectacular? A superstar? Then the bank would have lost out. Does this make sense? Would this make sense to the Head of the Lending Department? Does this sound familiar? *How many times have you been the 'perfect' candidate for a job, yet could never even get through the screening process?*

After week three and still no results, I called Olivia and told her to meet me in my office at 7:30 a.m. the next day, and bring the candidate's Professional Profile, which we had created from an intense questionnaire he had filled out regarding all his stellar accomplishments.

We went online and Googled the name of the bank. We then went to the bank's directory, clicked on the commercial lending department, and up popped a list of pictures and names of commercial lenders. We looked for the Head of Commercial Lending and next to him was his email and phone number. I then picked up the phone and called him. On the 3rd ring a Voicemail came on. I then left the following message:

"John, good morning, this is Jay Lang with Hudson Valley Career Development, and I am calling because I have an outstanding commercial lender and he is interested in discussing opportunities with your bank.

Then I started reading the Professional Profile:

"My candidate has:

- 20 years commercial banking experience
- Has opened territories in metro NY, NJ, and CT
- Has a book of business of over 150 clients
- Is formally credit trained
- Originates loans from $500k to $6M
- Consecutively does over $100M in loans on an annual basis

"Once again this is Jay Lang with Hudson Valley Career Development and we welcome the chance to speak with you. I can be reached at XXX-XX-XXXX repeat XXX-XX-XXXX. Thank you John, and have a wonderful day."

90 minutes later, while still discussing strategies, the phone rang and it was Human Resources from the bank.

HR: "May I speak with Jay Lang?"

Me: "Speaking."

HR: We understand you have a commercial lender, and we'd like to set up and interview ... but we can only pay 20% commission."

Me: "That works for me. When is a convenient morning to see our candidate"?

The interview went forward, the candidate was hired and we received our 20%. More importantly though, Olivia learned some great tools, a great strategy to circumvent HR and how to get directly to a decision maker.

This is yet another component in thinking like a head-hunter. Marketing yourself. Find companies that can use your talents. Start calling decision makers. Get yourself in front of them. Demonstrate your key skills and accomplishments. You just may be very surprised at the results.

As an exercise in the workshops I conduct, I tell the attendees that they have all been hired as recruiters. That they all have one, *and only one* candidate to place. This candidate has the same exact qualifications as they possess. When they get this person a job, their commission is what this person makes annually. This could be anywhere from $40,000 to $300,000. A very nice commission!

We then go over the steps that need to be taken to place this candidate: 1. Creating a strong Professional Profile to market the candidate. 2. Creating resumes and cover letters that are powerful and control all negative perceptions, while focusing in on an employer's needs. 3. Researching companies that align with our candidate's expertise and finding Decision Makers we can contact to present our candidate. 4. Practicing their prepared script.

The purpose of this exercise is to start thinking like a headhunter. Once you start doing what thousands of recruiters do on a daily basis, and earn a good livelihood doing it, you realize it's not so hard after all. It puts you in the driver's seat of your own destiny, and opens up many more opportunities than just looking for 'empty seat' positions online and submitting resumes; waiting for something to happen.

Thinking like a headhunter can turn your search for a job into a proactive marketing campaign. It will change your way of thinking from unemployed candidate to employed recruiter working to place an MPC—a Most Placeable Candidate. It can create a relentless drive in you in pursuit of that well rewarded annual commission you so highly deserve. And, it can get you back to work at a faster pace.

*MPC - 'Most Placeable Candidate'. This means as close to as perfect a candidate as possible. What is a perfect candidate? Someone who is happily employed. His numbers/status/accomplishments are A+, and he is not actively searching for a job.

(If you are unemployed, you are not *perceived* by other recruiters as a Most Placeable Candidate.) Of course this is *not true* but that is the perception by the industry. Change the perception (and your destiny) by using the powerful alternative tools described above to market yourself directly to Decision Makers.

CHAPTER 29

HUMAN RESOURCES—
WHAT DO THEY REALLY
DO AND THINK?

Human Resources is suddenly elevated to a level of a near godlike status when you are in a job search. Before becoming unemployed you barely gave them a thought. They were the department you primarily avoided, and for many of you, it was the department that called you in when you were let go. So, clearly there's not a lot of love there, and perhaps a lot of fear.

Today you are playing a game of cat and mouse with them. You are doing everything you can to satisfy their every whim, applying on line, not bothering them with phone calls (No Phone Calls Please!), dropping everything when they call you, going in for interviews when they tell you, feeling intimidated when you meet them, and in other words—bestowing on them far more power than they deserve.

Human Resources is probably the most misperceived department you will encounter. They are presumed to be 'experts' in recruiting. 'Experts' in interviewing. 'Experts' in ensuring that only the best of the best candidates get through the golden gates to be interviewed and hired. They hold the power to make major decisions, and if you bypass them, beware of the wrath that follows.

Now let's look at Human Resources objectively. In larger companies the head of Human Resources has a degree in Human Resource Management, where they spent a few years studying policies and procedures, hiring laws, ethics, payroll procedures, compliance and a host of other subjects and disciplines that have absolutely nothing to do with finding the very best candidate to meet an employer's needs.

(To be fair, there are some great Human Resource people, who know what they are doing when it comes to hiring, and are exceptional at knowing their companies' needs and filling positions with great hires—but this is the exception, not the rule.)

Along with all of this non-recruiting, non-hiring expertise comes another number to swallow. Most Human Resource personnel spend only a small percentage of their work week on the search/hire process. One Human Resource Generalist commented she typically spends less than 5% of her time recruiting. That's not a lot of time to sift through potentially hundreds of resumes. Even if they are using a recruiter, it may only be 10 or 20 resumes but nonetheless it's still a chore to actually read these resumes, try to make sense of them, where they would fit into the organization, and whether or not they are worthy to pass on to a Decision Maker.

Many large companies have a Talent Acquisition Specialists. These are people who actually spend their days looking for candidates. They are the next filtering source after the Applicant Tracking System. They may have to read potentially 100's of cover letters and resumes a day. They contact those that they perceive as a good fit, spend 15 to 20 minutes on the phone 'screening them' to be sure they are a worthy candidate to pass on to the next rung in the HR department, or perhaps a Decision Maker.

It's important to understand some things about Talent Acquisition. They are often employed on a contract basis ranging from 3 to 12 months. They may or may not be in the same discipline from job to job and many have only a few years of experience. As they jump from industry to industry, they generally don't know a lot about the real needs of the employer. This means *it's very hard for them to understand the value of someone who does not meet all the exact requirements of a job description.* Hence another obstacle in your job search.

Remember that exercise you had in primary school when you matched the chicken with the chicken coop? The duck with the pond and the farmer with the farmhouse? Well that same exercise is now deciding your fate. With highlighter pen in hand, whoever is screening your resume, is doing the same with your resume. Highlighting all those points that align with the job description, hoping to get enough to be able to get you up the ladder. If not enough yellow, you're out of luck. You may be the perfect candidate, but they just can't see it.

Think of the incompetency of this. Yet this exercise is carried out on a global basis and is used to find anyone from a janitor to a CFO. It's a scary when you realize the entire fate of your career is riding on this flawed process.

Ask anyone, what is HR's goal in selecting a candidate for an interview? Undoubtedly you will get an answer something like "trying to fill a position".

Actually that is their *secondary* goal. As we are all first interested in self preservation, their primary goal is making sure *they* look good when passing someone on, or at the very least not to be chastised for, a candidate that doesn't fit and is wasting a Decision Maker's time. Too many bad resumes passed along may even result in the loss of their job. So can you see why they are so reluctant to pass you on if you are not a perfect fit or at least very close to one. So here we have yet another road block.

There is yet another critical factor few address in the industry—effectively *presenting (or selling) of the candidate to the Decision Maker.*

Whoever has *screened* you, *highlighted* you in the "chicken and coop" matching exercise, and *called* you, now has to be able to effectively *present* you in such a manner that makes you look good (and them as well). Yet, just how good are people at communicating? How good are we at taking a boring lengthy resume, a boring cover letter, bits of scrambled notes from a phone call, and presenting all this information to impress a Decision Maker to actually interview you? Most of us are not very good at it, so when in doubt, what do we do? We don't. If it's all too hard to communicate, who you are, what you are and what you have to offer to the company, you won't be presented. Now, perhaps you are getting an idea of why you have sent out 30 resumes and have gotten nothing in return.

The impact on you and the company from all this? It has become the norm for companies on a global basis to have a 25% bad hire rate. These numbers are more realistically much higher. (A bad hire is considered anyone that leaves a company, other than through a downsizing or merger, within the first 2 years.) These bad hires equate to a loss of billions of dollars annually. Bad hires are the thorn in the side of companies and no matter what they do, they can't seem to stem the tide.

What can you do about all this? You are far better off realizing Human Resources are not effective in the hiring process. The brilliant author, trainer and arguably most respected name in the recruiting industry, Steven Finkel states in his book *Real Recruiting! "There is no doubt that they (Human Resources) are a serious impediment to effective hiring."*

Now that we understand Human Resources is a stumbling block to your employment, it's also time to understand, they seriously need *your* help!

They need your help in seeing you are a great fit, that you are a Most Placeable Candidate, that they will be given a pat on the back for finding you, and that they can easily and succinctly communicate you on to the next level.

Using the Professional Profile, a great cover letter, the Skills Alignment Matrix, the reader friendly resume, and the 3 Prong Approach, you will be helping them immensely. You will also be putting yourself ahead of the pack, and getting you closer to Decision Makers for an interview.

Refrain from placing the fate of your career into the hands of inept communicators who don't have your best interest in mind. Instead start helping them by providing your own dazzling marketing materials to more clearly exemplify your value to the company and put you more in control of the hiring process.

CHAPTER 30

DEALING WITH RECRUITERS AND HOW TO GET THEM TO WORK FOR YOU

It's is quite amazing how many people are intimidated by recruiters. When you were working, you might have gotten a call from one, felt somewhat flattered but dismissed them as an annoyance. Now things have changed. Today if you hear from one, you are at their beck and call. You may even make a 2 hour trip to the city to spend only 15 minutes in front of them for a casual get-to-know interview.

Don't be intimidated by them. They need you as much as you need them. Yes, the company is their client and is paying their fees, but without you, there is no compensation for them to reap.

Sadly there are not a lot of really good recruiters. Due to the ups and downs in the industry, when the going gets good, people from all kinds of industries decide to become recruiters. When it's bad, they bail. But deciding to become a recruiter is like just deciding to become anything that requires a lot of training, dedication, a knowledge of the business and the keen ability to work with people to put a very complicated deal together. One does not become a doctor, an engineer, a plumber or project manager overnight just by deciding to delve into this career.

For the last 15 years, a few trends throughout the industry have surfaced that need to be mentioned to help you understand who you are dealing with—the first one being, you'll be dealing with a number of rookies. Go online and look at jobs for recruiters. More and more they are seeking people from a particular industry to 'become' recruiters. They suggest that just because you were a software *engineer* you suddenly can transform into a top producing IT *recruiter*. Well just as a recruiter cannot instantly transform into an IT professional, it is very hard for the reverse to be true. Being a recruiter requires a substantial number of hard and soft skills that in the end very few firmly grasp—hence the great turnover in the business.

The other trend is companies are looking for recruiters with no more than 1 or 2 years of experience. The less you know the better? Right? No, the less experience you have the less commission we have to pay you per placement. Now this may be good for the recruiting firm (actually it's not, only being penny wise and pound foolish), but it certainly isn't good for you. Working with a poor recruiter is a bad decision, and can create yet another obstacle in getting you back to work.

How can a bad recruiter sabotage your job search and how can you tell the good ones from the bad?

A bad recruiter will barely get to know you. They may not even have a client relationship with a company. They may be sending out your resume to as many companies as possible, trying to get your name in first so they can get a fee. Many times they won't even call you, just upload your resume from a job board and send it out to as many companies as possible. The result of this? You are not presented in an effective manner to warrant an interview, you end up in the company's database, and you potentially lose a great opportunity. Then when you come across a good recruiter, it could be too late and he may not even be able to help you. Why? Companies you've already been submitted to will more than likely reject you. They don't want to get involved in a *procuring cause* lawsuit over fees. It's easier to just pass you up as a viable candidate. They also see you as *not* being in control of your number one priority—getting a job, and managing all your personal information. After all, as a professional, shouldn't you know who is brokering you? Managing you?

Always be in charge of who you're being presented by and to whom you are being presented. This is why having your resume online can work against you, as you don't know who or where you are being presented. You have relinquished all control of your own resume. Make sure you know all the companies you are being presented to by every recruiter you are working with.

A bad recruiter is evident on how little time they actually spend with you. 5 to 10 minutes? Do they know much about the job? Is the company their actual client? Do they ask you if you are working with other recruiters? Have you been submitted to a particular company? Have you applied online yourself? If they don't ask you these questions, they haven't been in the business very long and it may be best to move along.

How can you tell a good recruiter? They will want to know you inside and out. They will spend time getting to know you. Why you are looking for a job? How long you've been looking? What have you done in your search? Who have you applied to and when? What was your previous compensation? They may even want to know about your family. Is your spouse on board with your decision? Have you spoken to your family about the opportunity? They will ask many questions, as they themselves want to be well armed for questions about you from their clients; and they want to be sure of closing the sale by knowing as much about you throughout the process to avoid any last minute obstacles in the event an offer comes along.

Some recruiters may not even work with you if you are using other recruiters. If you are working with others, they'll want to know that you are aware of what companies you are being presented. They will tell you if a company is not their client, and be upfront with you. They will not try to wrangle another recruiter's company's name out of you, but they will make sure you keep everything between yourselves extremely confidential. There are many unscrupulous recruiters out there, and they will be on guard against them. They will also caution you on using other recruiters. If you're spread too thin, especially if you are in a niche market, the chances of crossing paths with another recruiter increases, and being presented to the same job by multiple recruiters is bad for everyone. Keep in mind, the number of companies you can be presented to is not an infinite number, and in many cases it may be very limited.

When it come to the interview process, a good recruiter will know exactly who is going to be interviewing you. Their style. Are they easy going or conservative? Their likes, dislikes. A good recruiter will even prep you for the interview and make sure you are at your very best before you walk through those doors. You are their product, and just as if you are prepping a car for resale, a good recruiter will do the same. Even down to what you are going to wear. Are you wearing a $200 suit that is five years old for a $100,000 job? Are your shoes polished? What happens if you run into a massive traffic jam on the way to the interview? A good recruiter leaves no stone unturned.

A bad recruiter will give you the address, time, and tell you to ask for Joan in Human Resources. They will not prep you, as they don't know how. They will not ask about your spouse, as they don't have enough business acumen to know that decisions such as a job are rarely made alone. They will not cover all the bases, and in the end, may actually sabotage your search.

A good recruiter knows he is not only making a sale but he is fostering a great relationship with his client company. He wants you at your finest, and will make sure of it. You are worth thousands of dollars to him, as well as his reputation in the industry. He will want to make sure you are going to make the best impression possible for yourself, and for him.

How to help a recruiter work for you

All recruiters need client companies. If a recruiter has clients, he can get job orders. The more clients the more job orders. However, recruiters can get too busy, or simply become complacent and stop mining for new clients. Yet, they know they need them, and it's also a constant thorn in their side to make those cold calls to companies; but just like you, nobody relishes the thought of making a cold call.

A cold call for a recruiter is using an MPC (Most Placeable Candidate) to market to a potential client. They use a great candidate to try show they can offer great people to a company. If they can get one job order, they can get more.

However, before a recruiter can make those cold calls to market an MPC, they first need a company. And, they need a Decision Maker in that company, not HR. Here's where you can come in. To find a Decision Maker in a company takes time. It's the research time that kills the recruiter. The calls take minutes, the research can take hours. So, you help the recruiter. Do the research. Find companies you want to work for. Find the department head, the hiring manager, the person that can make a decision and get their number. Get a dozen of these and line it all out for your recruiter. Company website, brief bio, etc. then give him your Professional Profile to market you. Talk to your recruiter and ask them if they will go along with this; many will jump at the chance if they see you as a viable candidate to market.

In conclusion, don't be intimidated by recruiters. Seek out good recruiters who can help you and avoid bad recruiters that can sabotage you. Listen carefully to the questions they ask you; they will tell a lot about the experience of the recruiter. Stay in control of your job search (and your resume) and know the companies you are being presented. Help the recruiter help you by looking for companies and contact numbers that he can use to market you

CHAPTER 31

THE FEAR OF OFFENDING

When we are unemployed, many fears surface. Fear of money, fear of not finding a job, fear of reaching out to people that could potentially help us. Then there is the fear of offending. The fear that if we call up or try to talk someone outside our circle, especially a Decision Maker, we will offend him and he will chastise us.

Of all fears, this is perhaps the one that causes the most grief and damage to unemployed job seekers. The fear of offending has the power to stop a career dead in its tracks. It has the power to paralyze the job seeker and will keep a seasoned professional from drawing on his past success in dealing with people. Now making a call to a decision maker has become a dreaded hurdle to overcome.

When employed, you never gave it a second thought. Got a problem? Call a decision maker. Now decision makers, suddenly through the power of the imagination—and self imposed intimidation—have risen to a godlike and unapproachable status.

This fear of offending is greater than the fear of being rejected, greater than the fear of staying unemployed. It paralyzes you and keeps you from moving ahead.

In reality, if you contact a Decision Maker and have a *professional* dialogue with them, you will likely *never* offend them or be chastised as your fears have dictated. In reality, they will more than likely be very impressed. They will see you as a professional that does what professionals do—takes the initiative, contacts Decision Makers and gets things done.

If you find yourself hesitating and being reluctant to do things such as reaching out to Decision Makers, ask yourself if that hesitation is coming from the fear of offending. If it is, pick up the phone and make the call—don't let the fear of offending get the best of you and sabotage your career.

CHAPTER 32

GETTING TO THE DECISION MAKER AND AVOIDING THE GATE KEEPERS

Getting to decision makers was rarely a problem when you were employed; yet when you find yourself sitting at home, alone with the computer and the phone, it becomes a different matter.

In workshops the question of "how to find (and reach) decision makers" often comes from the most seasoned professionals. *Previous* Decision Makers (such as yourself) now struggle to find the elusive Decision Maker. So getting to Decision Makers is both a psychological and a tactical matter.

The psychological aspect is that when you find yourself alone and unemployed, you are a fish out of water. Everything familiar suddenly seems foreign. So the thought of picking up the phone and talking directly to a decision maker suddenly has become the dreaded task. You brace yourself for the call. Are you worthy enough? Will you be offending them? Will you be dismissed with a grunt? What will HR think if you bypass them like this? Questions like these and more may be preventing you from even attempting the call.

The solution? *Reclaiming your professionalism.*

Grasp this concept: Realize that although you may not have the desk, the business card, the compensation and the business name behind you, you still *have* the years of experience that got you where you were. Recall all the Decision Makers you knew over the years. Would it really be an issue to call them as a professional and have a dialogue with them? Would you, as a former Decision Maker be put off? As the CEO of your own company *now,* would you be offended? Of course not. Pick up the phone and call.

Finding out who the Decision Makers are is easier now than it has ever been. Anyone can be found. Use your computer as the incredible tool it is; start going to the company's website. Search directories. Often it's right there on the site, pictures, contact numbers, email addresses. Google news about the company. Names of decision makers—make the news. LinkedIn has become an essential tool for recruiters in locating those once nearly impossible decision makers to find. Those in back office operations are suddenly right there in living color. Put yourself in a detective's state of mind and start your investigations.

As for getting past gatekeepers, get creative. Call before 8:00 a.m. and you are often sent directly to their voice-mail. Call at noon and the gatekeeper who keeps everyone away is suddenly replaced by the receptionist that lets everyone through. If you still can't get through, simply state something like "Is Elizabeth in?" If questioned, just tell them it's a personal call, it's pertaining to some business you are doing, etc.

A pathologist in the Job Club would refer to a complicated process in the lab she needed to address with a Hiring Manager—intimidating any gatekeeper and ultimately getting through to the Decision Maker every time. So use the expertise of your profession to break down barriers.

The logistics of getting to the Decision Makers differs with the company. If we are calling upon a Law Firm, then contacting a partner won't be as challenging as getting through to a VP of Marketing at a Multinational corporation. Some of these corporations are like fortresses and to penetrate them and reach an actual person can be a big challenge. Though it is not impossible. It is essential you put yourself into the same state of mind as when you were last employed. Consider it an assignment. Start getting creative.

Keep in mind, once you find a name, you can send your materials to him as a first step. From there, you have a very good reason to contact them—to insure receipt of the materials you posted, and as a courtesy follow up.

Think like a headhunter, be relentless in your pursuit of the people that can help you. Never lose sight of the fact that you are there to help them. That the fortress mentality of many corporations and the roadblocks and barriers that their Human Resources has created is only harming the company—by keeping the best of the best out. That their *blind faith* in ATS systems, contract Talent Acquisition personnel and Human Resource personnel inundated with work (that has nothing to do with hiring), can only be overcome by professionals such as you. Professionals who are creative and relentless at reaching their goals. And in this case, making contact with real Decision Makers, that can recognize your value and get you hired.

The ability to reach Department Heads, Hiring Managers, CEOs and CFOs of a company will put you miles ahead of the competition. Don't be intimidated by the process or the system or people who attempt to keep you out. Stay professional and realize you are actually 'helping the company' by getting to those that matter and addressing *their* needs. Keep in mind you are simply bypassing recruiters, and you may be very surprised when they actually thank you for calling them. Logistically, do your investigative research. Start calls early in the day, and be relentless in your pursuit of those that can make a real impact. Professionals find professionals and call professionals. That's the way the business world works.

CHAPTER 33

TALKING TO DECISION MAKERS—CLEARING UP PERCEPTIONS

Our perceptions of leaders can be very damaging. We often see them as smarter, more knowledgeable, more powerful than they actually are; this in turn naturally gives us an inferiority complex. Then when it's time to actually talk to them, we become a bundle of nerves.

This fear of Decision Makers runs deep even among those job seekers who have dealt with them their whole career. Why? It is the loss of one's professionalism that came with the loss of the job, and as time goes on, it continues to erode our confidence in dealing with those that can truly help us.

In workshops and in private counsel, I have met powerful leaders across many industries. Media, finance, IT, energy, telecommunications, entertainment, etc. CEOs, CFOs; titles and positions of people you would never think would be unemployed, or if they were, they'd have no problem in getting back to work immediately. Yet, there they are, just like the manager of the local bank—out of work.

Without fail, when a leader speaks out in the workshop, and presents himself to the other participants, three things happen. 1) The Leader - the Decision Maker, is really no different from the others; Decision Makers have the same insecurities and fears as everyone else. 2) When he is identified as the 'leader', *the face of the leader they have all been fearing*, everyone shakes their head, realizing that the perception they have created in their minds is a myth; he is just another person with problems just like them. 3) The group is surprised to find that the former Decision Maker is no more adept or skilled in the job search than they are; using the same traditional antiquated methods and running into the same roadblocks, and having the same problems in getting back to work—and talking to Decision Makers.

Stop to think about it. Talking to Decision Makers is what you did every day at your previous job. You were the 'go to person' within your sphere of influence. You were respected by them and they needed you. They needed your expertise. Nothing has changed. You are *still* the expert in your profession; you must continuously reclaim that which you have spent an entire career developing.

Take back the Professional within you. Live up to the status that you were recognized for in the workplace. Lose any intimidation you may have of them. Any inferiority complex. Start making direct contact with those that can make a difference, and start addressing Decision Makers as the professional you are. In turn you will find, they will respect you, appreciate your candor, and recognize you are a force to be reckoned with.

CHAPTER 34

SETTING UP DIALOGUES/ INTERVIEWS

At one time in history, women were not supposed to call men. All the pressure was on the man to make the call. Then everything changed. Women's lib opened the door in the 70's and everyone was free to call whoever they wanted.

In setting up dialogues and interviews with Decision Makers, the same applies. Who says you have to be asked? Getting in front of people at the company is a vital step in getting hired. 'You have to have interviews if you want to get hired'.

If you get a phone call after sending out your Professional Profile, and they are asking about seeing your resume, don't just tell them you will send it to them, ask them what prompted them to call you.

"What was it in the Professional Profile that caught your attention?"

Try to engage them into specifics. Create a dialogue. Then let them know you would be happy to bring the resume to them. That putting a face to a resume is advantageous and you'd love to meet them. Then ask them if they would they be available tomorrow to meet you, say at 9:00 a.m. in morning.

A very creative attendee to the job club, a former CFO of a manufacturing firm came up with a brilliant way of getting to Decision Makers and setting up his own interviews. After researching a company and finding the name and email of the person he wanted to meet, he would send them an email along with his Professional Profile, requesting an interview on a specific date.

Sometimes he would call and ask the Decision Maker's Executive Assistant if the Executive he was trying to meet was available that day. He would then follow up a few days before the "date of the interview" with a "confirmation of a scheduled meeting" with the Decision Maker.

Surprisingly he rarely received a response back from this. And if he did, it was to confirm the meeting as well. Then on the day of the scheduled meeting, he would show up at the company. If there was ever a question about who set up the meeting, he simply mentioned he had; that he had followed up with a confirmation of the meeting and thus assumed the meeting was still on. Inevitably he nearly always got in to talk with them.

Do we recommend this? If you have the ability and professional acumen to pull it off, absolutely. The point of the story is to prompt your own creativity in reaching Decision Makers. Sometimes it's just a matter of picking up the phone and calling. Whatever method you come up, keep your eye on the goal: Getting to the Decision Makers of an organization.

Remember, you have nothing to lose and the world to gain if you can consistently reach those that can make a difference. And, if done with confidence, professionalism, a consultant's frame of mind, and warm sincerity, you will impress them—and get that much closer to landing the job of your dreams.

CHAPTER 35

STRATEGIC NETWORKING— MAKE PEOPLE FEEL VALUABLE

It's been written about in volume of books, articles and blogs. You see it posted on walls at the Labor Department "Networking is the most effective way to find a job." Yet seminar after seminar, workshop after workshop at the Job Club, two factors consistently come up—for the long term unemployed, the majority of jobs are not found through networking, and most people are not very good at it.

Networking appears to work best for those who have have recently lost their jobs and have a good network to rely upon as it requires people. The more people you know the more effective. The problem is, your pool of contacts can be easily exhausted; after a few weeks of heavy networking, you may find yourself running out of contacts. Then what?

The other problem is, and the issue that is not covered very much at all is, people are just not very good at it.

The nature of networking in the job search is to get people to ultimately help you. However, most people are not good at asking for help. So they make a brief connection and quickly try to pass on their 'unemployment dilemma' and ultimately their resume to the people they meet; but nothing seems to happen. Why? Because, when you give people your 'unemployment problem' and your resume to people, you are putting them in a position of 'obligation' to you and 'risk' to themselves. Not a very comfortable place to be.

The people you 'dump' your resume onto will feel pressured to help you, and pressured to pass on your resume. You may think, what's wrong with passing on your resume? From their perception though, they may be putting themselves at risk in case you are a bad hire and it comes back to haunt them. You are also putting them in an awkward position of having to explain who you are and what you are, yet all they have is your resume—which is a very hard tool to convey verbally to others. It's easier to just not do anything, which is generally the case.

So how can we be better at networking? Never run out of contacts and better utilize every contact we meet?

When you meet people, whether in person or online, whether you know them or you don't, stop making the focus of the attention *you* and your lack of employment. People don't want to know about you and your woes, they want to talk about themselves. Yes, give them your 30 second movie trailer as described in chapter 9, but then focus in on them.

We highly recommend reading Dale Carnegie's book, *How to Win Friends and Influence People.* The premise of the book is to make other people feel valuable and important. Value is something all people crave. If they get it, they feel happy and are more likely to help you. If they don't get it, they'll feel indifferent to you and simply won't help you. So start making people feel valuable in all your networking.

When you come across an old acquaintance, or a new one, dig deep and show sincere interest in them. Avoid talking about yourself, and concentrate on them. Get beyond talking about business and get personal.

Countless times I have demonstrated this in workshops, and without a doubt it always makes the person not only feel good, but makes *me* memorable; which is the key to helping them help me. Below is an unabridged conversation between myself and an attendee at one of the workshops.

"So Daniel where are you from?"

"Right here in Rockland County."

"Really? And your parents are they from here?"

"No, actually they were raised in Brooklyn."

"Really? And so were their parents from Brooklyn as well?"

"Yes."

"And your grandparents?"

"No, actually they came from Russia."

"Russia? Wow, what year was that?"

"Well, it's a pretty fascinating story. My Grandfather escaped Russia right after the Revolution in 1917. Got across the border, made his way across Europe and got to America. I guess he was nearly killed crossing the border!"

Wow! So he escaped during that period! That is incredible!

Then I asked Daniel, "when was the last time you ever spoke about that?" "How do you feel now?" "How do you feel about me?"

He replied, "It's been years since I spoke about that, and never with a stranger. I feel great talking about it, makes me realize how special I am. And about you? I'll never forget this conversation".

I knew that would be his reply. Why? Most people never get past the surface of small talk. They end up talking about themselves, and as a result they never make the other person feel valuable. The result, the other person soon forgets them, and has no motivation to help them. *People help people that make them feel good.*

This conversation could easily have been turned into deeper questions about their career. How they got started. Did they always want to be an engineer? Did they build things when they were a kid? Was their father an engineer? Keep digging and you will see the enthusiasm on their faces as you bring up stories they haven't spoken about in years, if ever.

This can be done anywhere, with anyone. After you have made them feel valuable, ask them for their card, or a contact so you can stay in touch with them. You will be amazed how people will respond.

So what do you do if you feel the person is a worthwhile connection in the job search?

Send them an email within 24 hours and let them know it was great speaking with them and you really enjoyed hearing about their lives. In this case, I would have said to Daniel, "Your grandfather's escape from Russia was fascinating, I'd love to learn more."

Then end your letter by saying, "Hey, I've attached a profile of myself just to let you know a bit about myself. If anything comes your way that aligns with my background, I'd love for you to keep me in mind." Attach your Professional Profile, *not* your resume.

By the nature of the Professional Profile, it isn't screaming "I need a job!" It's showing them who you are in a matter of seconds. They see you've got an amazing career in mining and exploration with some distinguished accomplishments. Memorable stuff. So in the event that something comes up within their circle of influence, you can be pretty sure they will say:

"You know, I met someone who is a mining engineer. Real nice guy with some great accomplishments. Let me get the bio he put together, and I'll get it to you".

The other advantage to this approach to networking is, it's very easy. *It's especially helpful to those that shy away from networking events due to their dislike of meeting strangers and creating 'small talk'.* This approach is simply all about them. Just keep asking questions, show sincere, genuine interest in them, and then stand back and let them talk.

So take your networking to a whole new level by digging deep, making others feel valuable, and making yourself memorable. Resist the urge to talk about yourself or giving out your resume. Follow up, stay in touch, use your Professional Profile, and start reaping the benefits of sincere fellowship with others.

CHAPTER 36

JUST PICK UP THE PHONE AND CALL

The shortest distance between two points is a direct line. In this case the phone.

There are times whether through frustration with the process of applying online and sending resumes, you've grown weary of receiving rejection letters, or you are so fed up with playing the traditional game of trying to get through Applicant Tracking Systems and appeasing Human Resources, that you just start picking up the phone and start calling.

When I first arrived in Australia in the 1990's, I sent dozens of resumes to companies. In those days the internet wasn't yet at the stage it is now, and going 'snail mail' was the norm. Lengthy CV's in colorful thick binders were sent out weekly. The results were a continuous flow of rejection letters, so many I took to wall papering my small office with them. Then I got fed up.

One morning I'd had enough and instead of looking for 'empty seat' positions I grabbed a phone book and started looking for companies in my area of expertise. Then I started calling. Soon one phone call led to another. I was usually getting through to Decision Makers, and I was having dialogues with heads of companies within minutes that I had been unable to obtain in 6 weeks of sending out the traditional materials. The results? One Decision Maker referred me to another Decision Maker, I was invited in for an interview, and was hired a few days later.

Before my arrival in Hawaii, I had sent out dozens of resumes as well. The results? Of course dozens of rejections. Then I started picking up the phone and calling. The results? 2 offers after 2 interviews.

Prior to coming to New York, months were spent looking for jobs on all the traditional job boards and shooting out an endless number of resumes. The responses as you can guess, were dismal and depressing. Then in a last ditch effort, I jumped on a plane and flew to New York and checked into a hotel. Early the next morning I picked up the phone directory and started calling companies. By the 3rd phone call I had landed two interviews. The next day I had interviews and was subsequently given two offers.

This same story is heard time and again in the Job Club workshops. Job seekers getting fed up with the entire process, and instead just reaching for the phone and calling. And the results? The ratio of interviews to calls in comparison to interviews to send outs is almost always substantially higher.

Yes, sometimes it may seem impossible to get through in any other means than the traditional approach, then again, when you are at the end of your rope, desperation calls for drastic measures. In this case, just start picking up the phone and see if it will start working for you. You may be very pleasantly surprised by the results!

CHAPTER 37

GOING DOOR TO DOOR

Just as picking up the phone in Chapter 36 can have excellent results, so can simply knocking on doors. This is especially true with disciplines in such fields where groups of the same professionals set up business. Lawyers, accountants and banks, are some that come to mind. Armed with your Professional Profile, make the rounds. Introduce yourself and try to get to the Decision Makers. The Professional Profile makes an excellent calling card at this time.

An important key is your ability to walk in and create a warm relationship with the 'gatekeeper'. Usually the receptionist. Let them know what you are there for. If they are busy, ask if you can wait. Be persistent and be professional. If you are unable to get through, leave them your Professional Profile and take their card. Let them know you will be following up in a few days. Be friendly, warm and courteous.

Tony, a bank examiner, whose expertise was compliance and auditing, and who had made it a passion to learn all the new rules and laws, policies and procedures introduced after the banking crises, could not get a job, nor even an interview, though he had sent out dozens of resumes to banks and financial institutions. In class one day, I asked him how many of the banks out there are applying the new rules to their auditing.

"Not many at all!" he responded.

"What happens if they don't apply the new rules?"

"They will be considerably fined!"

I then explained that this scenario presented him with a perfect opportunity. That it could be highly productive to contact heads of banks, ask them if they are applying the new auditing laws, and if they aren't, what the consequences could be.

He then started doing exactly that, with excellent results. Knocking on bank doors and working his way up to those that mattered. Within a few months he was hired by a major New York City bank, and 3 years later he is still gainfully and happily employed.

It has become the norm rather than the exception, for those that attend the workshops and clients we have worked with, that knocking on doors, increases your chances of getting interviews dramatically. Sure it can be nerve wracking at first, yet once you realize that your value to the company and what can be achieved by meeting face to face with Decision Makers, without all the gatekeepers of the traditional job search, you may find yourself knocking on far more doors, landing far more interviews, and receiving far more offers than you ever imagined.

CHAPTER 38

A RESUME STATE OF MIND

The resume state of mind refers to thinking of yourself only as it relates to the last 1 or 2 jobs you had, especially as it relates to your resume. As most HR and recruiters usually only scan the last few jobs you had, thinking those are the only ones with relevance, it's easy to also fall into this trap, and either discount or totally eliminate all the careers you had that created the professional you are today.

A highly successful account manager in the New York fashion industry in the 1990s, transitioned into a full time mom. After ten years, she started a career in medical device sales and did a phenomenal job of generating over 400 new accounts in a 3 year period. Then she lost her job and was floundering. "I only have three years experience in sales, and with ten years as a full time mom, how am I ever going to get back my career back?"

She had entirely deleted her fashion industry sales experience not only off her resume, and her Professional

Profile, but also out her her mind. All the millions of dollars in revenue she had generated, all the accounts she had established, all the amazing work she had done in NYC, gone. Yet when questioned about her experience in the fashion industry, she lit up with enthusiasm. When asked if she could still generate such revenue and open new accounts, she replied "Of course, I did it in medical devices, I can do it with anything I set my mind to."

A CPA, out of work for 5 months came to me with over 30 years experience in a multitude of industries. His last few jobs had been with private CPA firms. His resume was dated back to the 1990s, was three pages long, and consisted of companies where he had worked followed by a list of boring responsibilities. No numbers, no names, no accomplishments—just that he created financial statements and the like.

Quickly scanning his resume, I noticed he had worked in the music industry in New York. Intrigued, I asked him:

"Did you ever meet any famous musicians"?

"Yes, actually I was CPA and accountant for a *very famous* 'rock star' couple for three years in New York City.

"Why isn't *this* on your resume?"

"I didn't want to date myself" he replied.

I explained to him that what he *was, and still is*, a highly distinguished and established accounting professional. The fact that he had worked for arguably the most famous couple in the musical world with a reputation as being very wealthy and shrewd—that *that* was all he needed! Needless to say, when he started telling people of his accomplishments, he was back to work within a few months.

Lose the resume state of mind that creates in your head the perception that you are only as good as your last few jobs. In reality you are as good as all those accomplishments you succeeded in; and are what make you what you are today. Bring them out in the Professional Profile, without any dates, and they will be as relevant as the day they were created.

CHAPTER 39

LINKEDIN AS A RESEARCH TOOL

It has never been easier to find, gain access to, or learn who the Decision Makers are than now. LinkedIn has become the single largest gold mine for recruiters in their hunt for great candidates. The elusive Decision Makers are revealed, in full living color along with their career history and background. And just as recruiters use the site, you can also use it the same way to find those department heads so vital in your strategy of marketing yourself.

Simply conduct a search for a potential target company and up pops everybody linked to the company. Remember all you need is that one name of the decision maker and that department. If you happen to be linked to them through your own network of contacts, reach out to them. Use your professional acumen. What is going to be more beneficial? A warm personal call first with your materials? Then a short note to them letting them know you sent them a Professional Profile for their perusal? Or perhaps a direct contact of yours is closely linked to them in the same company and you can have them forward it in to them. Whatever tactic you use, grasp the power that lies there in this gold mine of decision makers so easy to access.

As a marketing tool

If you are going to be using social media for marketing of yourself online, LinkedIn is the one site that we recommend for its safety and security. Sure you may get asked by a stranger in Nigeria to be part of your network, but simply refuse them. Sure millions of people throughout the world will be able to see who you are, yet with your ability to control all personal information, it's very limited in scope for them. LinkedIn does a good job of keeping the bad guys out, and keeping the site highly professional.

We recommend in your marketing to post a picture of yourself. Today, a site without a picture tells everybody else you are either social media shy, or you have something to hide. In any event, it isn't going to help you. Put your picture up. You'll get more invites and more people will accept you. If you are wondering what type of picture, simply look at the other pictures on the site, and determine which type best fits your profession and character.

Use your Professional Profile for the summary of who you are. This is great for recruiters looking for candidates with your skill sets, and tells people what you are, what you have to offer and doesn't leave them guessing. And once again, they don't have to sift through a lot of useless information, nor be sidetracked by perceptions that may hurt you. It's also a very safe way of marketing yourself if you are employed. In addition, you can add in the summary: 'Willing to discuss opportunities'. Be sure to include your email address as well, so that they can link with you immediately.

As a living breathing bio that rocks

LinkedIn allows others to add recommendations and referrals from your contacts. Build these up, and help build others up. It's your way of gaining credibility within your industry and community. Just as you look at the reviews for any product you buy, any restaurant you plan to visit, potential employers will look at your site to see how strong are your recommendations. You can even state these in your Professional Profile and resume. Realize that 250+ endorsements for marketing and sales skills from LinkedIn can look very impressive to those making the decision whether to interview you or not.

Additional tools

Put your LinkedIn address as part of your letterhead on your resume. It instantly tells us you are current, proud to display your value, and you are out there in the social media world and comfortable with it.

The jobs posted on LinkedIn are current and real. Given the cost of posting a job on Linked, you can rest assure they are authentic. Some job seekers from the Job Club have had excellent results with this medium in getting interviews and jobs.

You can join groups within LinkedIn within your industry or those industries you are interested in. Start commenting on these sites and watch your contacts soar. You can even start your own group and add credibility that way.

Stay current. As a member of LinkedIn, check in daily for messages to you (or have them forwarded on to your phone). Spend at least 15 minutes a day on the site. It's a great motivator, and it keeps you in that state of mind that there is a world out there of the employed professional, and you are only one interview away from it. As your contacts grow, and your recommendations grow, your confidence will also increase.

As all jobs are potentially temporary, even when you become employed, you must always stay abreast of hiring trends within your industry. LinkedIn can keep you in the radar of people looking for your skill sets, and opportunities may surface just when you need them—like when that new regional manager starts to clean house, and you're feeling pressure.

There are now classes given by libraries, colleges and your local labor department that will get you started using LinkedIn for those unfamiliar with the medium. I highly recommend taking one of these to get you started as soon as possible.

Keep in mind, if you are not on LinkedIn, and can't be seen, you just may not exist to a large number of people who could be helping you; internal and external recruiters, professional associates, anyone that may be looking for your set of skills. It is a norm these days for recruiters to go straight to LinkedIn to view your profile. If they can't find you, they may more than likely just pass you by.

So use LinkedIn as your window to the working world. As your source to view an almost unlimited number of people that may help you. As a great tool to get inside companies that was never possible before. Then market yourself. Create perceptions that will benefit you. Create an impact by building up your endorsements and recommendations. Join groups and start being recognized. Start writing articles that raise your profile and get you noted for your expertise. LinkedIn is not a cure all for the job seeker, yet it is a powerful tool that should be in every job seeker's tool box.

CHAPTER 40

IT'S STILL A NUMBERS GAME— JOB TRACKER

Good recruiters know their numbers. Their metrics. They know that if they want to make a placement it may take scouring 50 resumes. From these resumes perhaps there are 6 candidates he wants to speak with; from these he may send out 3 for an interview. From these 3 he's fortunate if 2 secure a second interview. Perhaps from these 2, 1 will get hired.

It's the same with you. No matter how good you are and how much more the tools in this book have improved your job search skills, it's still very important to keep track of your numbers. You need to know that you have to hit x number of companies to get x number of phone interviews to get x number of face to face interviews to get x number of second interviews to get x number of offers.

Of course it's highly possible to apply to one job and get hired, but with the competition today, we are seeing among those we train and coach that in all likelihood it takes applying to a number of companies to finally land that job.

Using the tools described in this book, your numbers will substantially improve. Typically the job seekers that come to us have sent out 100 resumes. From this they have had 4 or 5 phone interviews and perhaps 2 face to face interviews with no results. With great marketing tools and improved interview skills, they have watched their numbers improve drastically. Yours will too.

We have provided below the Job Tracker which will help you document your metrics and allow you to keep track of your progress. Use it. If you start to get down because you haven't gotten the results you expected, look at your numbers. Perhaps you need to market yourself to 10 companies to land an interview and you've only contacted 5.

Think like top recruiters do. Use numbers to track your progress, and help you move closer to that job you want.

JOB TRACKER:

Job Tracker Activity Chart

Dates	Com-pany Name	Position Applied to	Source of Job Opening	Decision Makers Contact Name & Title	Phone	Email	LinkedIn
Pro Profile Sent	FU Call Made	Send SAM	Phone Inter-view	F-to-F Interview	Thank You Sent	Second FU Call	Notes

CHAPTER 41

DEALING WITH REJECTION

The fear of rejection can prevent us from acting, which in turn can prevent us from reaching our dreams. In this case, the potential job of a lifetime. We have discussed that using the tools from this book, and not just 'white knuckling it' are keys to overcoming the fear of rejection.

Being rejected is the cold naked truth. It can be a lonely feeling knowing that someone has rejected us. So we take it personally and we start retracing our steps to see where 'we' went wrong. Yes, it's important to analyze our previous performance, but the key is to learn from it and move on, not dwell on it and allow it to further erode our confidence.

Putting things into perspective as for what we are actually doing in the job search, and what it essentially is, are powerful tools in dealing with rejection. What are we actually doing? We are marketing the services we excel in to the highest buyer. What is the job search all about?

It's a business transaction. There is no need to take it personally.

Keeping this in mind can take it out of a subjective, self-blaming state of mind to a business state of mind, to keep pushing on, improving our methods, and realizing that there are buyers out there for our unique services, we just need to find them.

Rejection can be a great motivator as well.

It can propel you to finally get that college degree you've meant to get all these years but keep putting off. It can motivate you to stop an endless send out of applications online, to picking up the phone and calling the Decision Maker. It can broaden your horizons—that job in Alaska, just may be a great opportunity after all. Rejection, like its twin, failure, are potential destroyers, or they are simply doors that are shut which can open up to greater opportunities.

In looking back on your life, how many times has a failure or a rejection turned into a blessing in disguise? It's the way our lives are formed and the ways and means that every great artist, scientist, inventor, and entrepreneur has finally succeeded.

So when you get rejected by a potential employer, learn from it. Realize it's only a business transaction. Take it for what it is—simply a temporary roadblock that with tenacity, and a refusal to never give up in our competitive business environment, you will overcome it and continue to move on regardless of the setbacks.

PART IV

THE INTERVIEW AND
THE OFFER

Now that you've landed the interview, the ability to demonstrate in 'real time' all your skills, talents, and accomplishments—and how they align with a company's needs, all comes together in a battle of wits, personality and negotiating for more.

CHAPTER 42

THE GOAL IS GETTING INTERVIEWS

In order to land a job, you first need to get interviews.

Ask any job seeker what they are trying to do and they will reply

"Trying to get a job".

The problem with this approach is that by focusing on the end goal, they lose track of the importance of the process; that is, you have to get interviews first. Interviews are the lifeline to getting jobs. No interview—no job.

The primary problem with today's antiquated job search of 'post and pray', shooting off an endless number of resumes to jobs found on job boards, is that it results in very few interviews.

Consistently, across the board, those that only apply online have only a 3-5% success rate in getting a phone screening or a possible interview.

Start using the tools learned so far in this book to start generating interviews. Continuously use the 3 Prong Approach when applying to jobs to get your materials to Decision Makers. Make it your profession to get to those that can make a difference, and stop relying on Human Resources to get you back to work. Securing interviews should always be your primary focus.

CHAPTER 43

ACE THE INTERVIEW AND YOU GET THE JOB

Just as you can't get a job without *getting* an interview, you can't get the job without *acing* the interview.

An interview is like the marriage after the wedding. A couple will spend months planning a wedding, making sure all is perfect down to the smallest detail—with barely a thought that the event is going to lead to a lifetime of commitment.

In a similar way, you spend hours, weeks, months scanning for jobs online, applying to countless jobs, sending out hundreds of resumes. You make sure all is perfect—then you get an interview and you decide to wing it!

Perhaps it comes in a phone call from an unknown number driving down the highway—and suddenly you find yourself talking to a panel of several interviewers during rush hour traffic. You're not prepared. You're not even sure who they are, as you've sent out so many resumes. What are the chances of your acing that interview?

No matter who you are, or what position you have occupied, prepping for the interview, is a critical component in landing your job. There is no faking it till you make it here. Faking is for those that don't want to win.

Even if you are working with a recruiter, it is shocking how many recruiters will send their candidates out with little more than a brief description of the company, with minimal prepping of who they they will be meeting. So if you're working with a recruiter, insist they prep you and provide as much information as possible about the company, its culture, who you will be meeting, and what are the key points that the employer is looking for in their decision making process.

Work with family and friends, work with a job coach, or contact us to help prep you for your interview by asking you challenging questions that require you to think on your feet and demonstrate how you are the best fit for that job.

What you have to internalize is that, after you've done all your hard work in getting to the interview, there is still a lot of work ahead before you have that offer securely in hand. Like a warrior going into battle, you must have mind, body and spirit zoned into the moment, your professionalism securely intact, and your goals focused to find out the real issues at hand, and to prove without a doubt, you are the person for the job.

The following chapters will prepare you for the interview process. We suggest reading these chapters a number of times, and especially before every interview until they are fully absorbed and become the tools you will reach for throughout the interview process.

CHAPTER 44

DON'T PICK UP THAT PHONE!

We will make this short and simple. Don't pick up the phone when it rings if it's a number you are unfamiliar with. Let it go into your voicemail. It is *not* an emergency. You can be assured that if it is a recruiter, HR or someone else interested in talking to you about a job, they *will* leave a message.

If you do happen to pick up the phone and you're not prepared, simply tell them you are unable to talk at the moment and when would be the best time to call back.

This may seem like a small factor in the job search, but it goes back to the importance of *working the process.* Skip a step and lose an opportunity. That phone call may be your first initial contact with that company. If you are rushed, frazzled, nervous, distracted or not prepared, you could blow the opportunity of a lifetime. First impressions are crucial; you only have one chance to make a great first impression.

Keep in mind, being in control of the job search and in control of yourself is paramount. You cannot control outside influences in a public setting.

During one Job Club session, a phone rang and out rushed the anxious job seeker into the lobby to answer it. In this public setting, he was suddenly confronted by a very noisy, incoherent man screaming at police, furniture being kicked against the wall, and bystanders all around panicking. Needless to say he didn't get the job nor even a chance to set up a face to face interview. Don't let this happen to you.

If the phone rings, let it go into your voicemail and call back when you are ready, calm and fully prepared. Stay in control of your job search at all times!

CHAPTER 45

PREPARING FOR THE INTERVIEW— KNOW THE COMPANY

This is nothing new, and by instinct, you know that preparing for the interview by learning all you can about the company is power. But go the extra mile. The time put into this research can give you the edge on others you are up against.

Google the company's *news*. This will often reveal far more recent and subtle changes that's going on with the company. A quote from the CFO made a few years ago, can be a very powerful way to gain favor. Your observation that the company has plans to expand will show you have a good handle on things. The more you know, the better off you are. People like to know you have taken a keen interest in the company; and not just when they started, how many employees they have, etc., which anyone can get off the company website.

Read and print out the company's mission statement. This will supply you with values and company standards even those interviewing you may not know. One Job Club member pulled out the mission statement in an interview and started talking about how she aligned with their core values. The VP of Marketing of 5 years, asked "Where did you get this, I've never seen it before?" "Off your website." She replied.

She is convinced this small act of due diligence impressed the top Decision Makers so much that it landed her the job. Incidentally, her Professional Profile and Skills Alignment Matrix were so powerful, *she didn't even use a resume for this job*. She landed her dream job, Director of Sales at a company, with a compensation package of 25% more than she imagined.

When you are setting up the interview with Human Resources or a recruiter, ask them specifically who you will be meeting. What departments are they with? What is typically their style of interviewing? Lots of technical questions? Behavioral type? Mainly dialogue?

It may surprise you the amount of information Human Resources is willing to give you at that point. Why? Because now that an interview has been requested by a department head, Human Resources knows it has so far done a good job and they would love for you to be hired. Now they are subtly switching over to your side and will start helping you—if asked. Human Resources wants to fill the position. They want to move on and be recognized as doing a good job. So use this window of time to let them help you.

Then go to LinkedIn and start doing research on who you will be meeting. Here is where you can usually find a considerable amount of information about each individual. How long have they been at the company? What previous roles have they played in other companies? Are they from that industry or have they transitioned over? Are they social media conscious and have lots of endorsements and recommendations; or are they 'socially media shy' and have only 15 connections? Are they closely linked to you through other members? If so, you may want to contact someone you trust and ask them about the individual.

Arming yourself with this information will help you in a number of different ways. By learning about those interviewing you, and even what they look like, can greatly relieve you of the interview jitters. You may see that Director of Sales has actually only been with the Bank a few years and came over from the Auto industry. Now suddenly your transition into banking from pharmaceuticals isn't so far fetched as you thought. Or you find the CMO also has a consulting business on the side. So now your fears that your side business is going to be a bone of contention, suddenly has become an asset.

One job club member discovered the CEO who was going to be interviewing him had written a book, and had his own website as well. He researched the site and started reading excerpts from the book. By the time he walked into the interview, he was ready to use this information to his advantage. Knowing that writing a book is a huge endeavor, he congratulated the CEO on the book, and told him he had shared it with a number of associates in the same industry, and even asked him what his favorite times to write were. This was an instant ice breaker and the first 10 minutes of the interview were all about the CEO. Later in the interview he brought up the 'cleanness' of the CEO's website, and this launched the conversation into how they might improve the current website at the company. More chances for the candidate to demonstrate his value to the company.

Another Job Club member in their research on LinkedIn found out the position he was interviewing for was still being held by the outgoing Director of Training. He saw that the director had been with the company for 20 years and had advanced through the ranks by sheer determination. When he was being interviewed, he detected from her demeanor that she was the challenging one, out of the four interviewers. When asked later if he had any questions, he turned his attention to her—asking how long she had been doing the job and how she transitioned into such a role. She told him she had started as Teller and gradually became Director. She noted that she had created the department singlehandedly, and she would be the one training the incoming Director.

Getting her to talk about her role changed her demeanor and her mood changed. He then took it one step further and applauded her in going from Teller to Director, an accomplishment few have achieved, and then asked the group

"How can anyone be able to possibly fill her shoes?"

At this point the CFO stated "That is the challenge! Linda has done such a fantastic job, how can we possibly fill them?"

With this, Linda was all smiles, and the entire interview ended on a very pleasant note.

Do your research. Learn about the company, and even more important, learn about the people you are going to be meeting. Then use it. Your efforts will not go unnoticed, and it will put you far ahead of those that have failed to thoroughly plan for the interview.

CHAPTER 46

DECISION FATIGUE— GET IN EARLY!

The New York Times published an article by John Tierney August 17, 2011 in which 3 men doing time in Federal Prison came up for parole. One at 8:50 a.m., one at 3:10 p.m. and the last one at 4:25 p.m. All had been convicted of similar crimes and all had been given similar sentences. Can you guess which one was paroled?

"Prisoners who appeared early in the morning received parole about 70 percent of the time, while those who appeared late in the day were paroled less than 10 percent of the time!"

The article goes on to explain that when our brains are fatigued by making decisions all day, we have a tendency to react in 2 different ways. One is to make impulsive decisions and the other is, as the article states: "Do nothing. Instead of agonizing over decisions, avoid any choice."

Now let's put this in perspective to the interview process. If your interview is set for 3:00 p.m. what is the likelihood the interviewer could be suffering from decision fatigue?

From the research done on decision fatigue, it appears it is very high. So why take the chance? You may be completely alert for the interview. Say all the right things and be the perfect fit for the job. Yet, if the head of the department is too overwhelmed to make a decision, and the easiest thing for him to do, is do nothing, your future career has been hijacked by decision fatigue.

So when Human Resources is scheduling your interview time, aim for the earliest times of the day. Even if you have to make up an excuse that you have another appointment that day, if the research is to be believed, the odds are heavily in your favor to get in early when the decision maker's minds are clear, unfatigued and ready to take in all you have to offer—and make a favorable decision in your favor!

CHAPTER 47

DON'T THINK!
OVERCOMING THE
INTERVIEW JITTERS

With 10+ years in marketing and shipping logistics and an MBA, John had no problem in getting interviews. In fact he had had 15 interviews in the 3 months before I met him. He just couldn't get past the first or second interview phase. By the time he joined the group, he was angry, distressed and it showed. He had also developed a habit of tapping his fingers, adjusting his shirt and rambling on whenever he was asked to speak in the workshop. He was obviously quite nervous when speaking in a group setting. Not good in today's world of interviewing!

Sound a little familiar? Nearly all the people I meet are nervous going into an interview. And you can't blame them. Most haven't been in interviews in years, and if they have, most haven't done very well at it; remember they are not professional interviewees. So after all their work of getting past the screening process, finally getting an interview, doing all their homework, hours of prepping for the interview, and finally ready to meet with decision makers for this ideal job—they blow it with the interview jitters.

Being nervous for an interview works against you. It puts your mind and body in a fight or flight state. Adrenalin is being released, rushing into your brain, and causing it to literally start short circuiting. Your brain could really care less about the interview; it just wants to get out of there. And, the sooner the better. Being nervous puts your mind into that state where short term memory alludes you, your mind goes blank, and everything start working against you.

All those wonderful things you planned to tell the interviewer about yourself suddenly are not there, it's just a jumbled mess in your mind. The questions they are asking; against your best judgement, you find yourself replying with answers that end up going nowhere and get you even deeper into trouble. You forget to ask your planned questions, and even if you do, you still can't focus.

So what can you do about these harmful jitters that are destroying your ability to ace the interview and get you back to work? The answer is surprisingly simple: *Don't think!*

Your job now is to focus on the moment. To listen. To make mental note of cues, that you can use to guide the conversation in your favor and align you with the needs of the company. Your mind must clear and focused at all times; not clouded with a lot of facts and figures or canned responses, or anxiety created by projecting ahead about the compensation.

The nervous marketing and shipping logistics professional mentioned in the first paragraph, later stated to the class, that while walking into his 16th interview, he glanced at his notebook from class briefly and saw scribbled across two pages "Don't Think!" He then went on to say that is was determined not to, and he didn't. Instead he listened strategically, watched for cues, removed himself from his self consciousness—and ultimately turned the interview into a powerful and productive dialogue between professionals—and got the job! Overwhelmed with joy, he credited '*not thinking*' as the primary factor that allowed him to listen and think objectively, to ultimately prove that he was the perfect candidate for the job.

So clear your mind. Learn to focus on the moment and don't think!

CHAPTER 48

EMPLOYER/EMPLOYEE VS. CLIENT/CONSULTANT

We typically think of our relationship with employers as an 'employer/employee' one. This relationship naturally puts the employer above us in status. That they are the ones that choose us. They are the ones that pay us. They are the ones we depend upon.

Once you become unemployed, that status now changes to 'employer/*unemployed - employee*'. This now puts the employer at an even higher status level which psychologically puts us at an even greater disadvantage. We see them as more powerful than us. We feel we must cater to their every whim and they are totally in control.

What can we do about this? We can change the way we perceive the relationship and in turn psychologically put us at an advantage in every point of contact with the 'employer'.

Stop thinking of it as an 'employer/employee' relationship and think of it as a 'consultant/client' relationship. You are the consultant and the employer is the client. They have a problem and you are there to find out what it is and solve it.

With a consultant's mindset, you can now approach the employer in every endeavor in the job search. From marketing yourself, to the interview, to negotiating compensation, you will find yourself more in synch with the professional you are and what your purpose is all about; finding out what an employer's needs are and demonstrating you can satisfy them.

CHAPTER 49

STAY SUCCINCT, TO THE POINT, AND SHUT UP

Without a doubt, this is one of the hardest things for people to do. When asked a question they just can't cut out the fluff and stick to the facts.

A typical response to the simple question "why did you leave your last employer?" often leads to a long winded story that ends up sabotaging the interview even before it begins.

"Well, the direction of the company and the way I thought it should be going weren't in alignment. I had numerous discussions with my boss and in the end it was decided we should part ways. Then there was the 2 hour commute every day that was killing me, and having to get home late was not doing my family any good. I was so tired on the weekends that I couldn't watch my handicapped son play soccer, who incidentally is getting a scholarship to attend The University of Maryland. Real nice area. Have you been there?"

Besides annoying the listener with information that doesn't pertain to the job search, not answering the question, and furthermore wasting precious interview time—what has the listener, the interviewer really heard?

That this person bucks the company and won't go along with the program. He is unwilling to commute. He lacks astuteness in talking about personal matters and has a handicapped son that may keep him from work. Finally, that he may not last as he seems to be thinking of moving to Maryland to watch his son play soccer.

Interviewers love it when you ramble on and on. A Director of HR stated at a workshop, "We intentionally stay silent after a candidate answers a questions. People can't stand silence. So inevitably the person will start talking again, and soon they will be giving us far more information than we could ever have ever gotten—and usually it just ends up burying them."

Concentrate on being succinct and direct in your responses to their questions. Answer the question and then shut up. Your ultimate purpose is to demonstrate who you are and how it addresses their needs. The rest is all irrelevant fluff—and dangerous territory. Loose lips surely do sink ships.

CHAPTER 50

PHONE INTERVIEW STRATEGIES FOR SUCCESS

The goal of the telephone interview is to take it to the next level, getting a face to face interview.

The problem with most telephone interviews is that they can easily put you at a disadvantage. However, there are a number of strategies you can use to assure success.

Be the one to make the call. When HR calls you to set up the interview, ask them if it would be acceptable for you to call them. This puts you at the advantage because when the time to make the call comes, you are focused and prepared. If they are to call you at 9:00 a.m. and you are ready to go at the time, and the phone doesn't ring, you are put at a disadvantage. The clock ticks to 9:05. Then 9:07. With every minute that passes, your focus erodes and anxiety replaces it. If they haven't called by 9:20, chances are your bladder has and off to the bathroom you go. Then the phone rings. This may sound funny, but it's not. It's a potential sabotage to your future career. All because of a late phone call. However if you were to have made the call, this would have never happened.

If they insist on calling you, and it gets to 9:10 and the phone still hasn't rung, *call* them up. Tell them you are confirming a telephone interview at 9:00 and you want to make sure it is still scheduled. Your time is valuable. Don't let others leave you hanging, and take you out of control. Remember you are running a business here, and good business etiquette is to be on time.

Stand up, do not sit. Standing (and slightly pacing) while on the phone changes the entire tone of your voice. You are more robust and sound more confident. It increases circulation and your brain is getting more blood. You ability to listen and think is sharper and enhanced. You will feel better and be more in control, so get out of the chair, and onto the stage.

Watch your pace, pause, listen for the cues ... and smile. We are at a disadvantage over the phone. You cannot read body language or facial expressions. As these count for nearly 50% of our communication cues, you are missing out on a lot of social cues.

Tone of voice and words are all you have to rely upon. So you have to be tuned into both yours and the interviewer's nuances and cues at all times. Your pace at which you naturally speak should be slowed down to a leisurely pace. Accent it with pauses between important points you are addressing. This allows the interviewer to interrupt and ask you questions, or grunt a nod of approval. It also turns it into a dialogue. A natural flow of information between two people, and not just you talking into a void.

If you are rushing through your answers to their questions, keep in mind they are probably taking notes, so give them time to write things down as well. Listen for cues, pause and slow it down. Smile. This changes your tone of voice and naturally releases endorphins that will make you less tense and feel better. You might even have fun.

Most importantly, have your Professional Profile right in front of you. Your Professional Profile is now your best friend. When you are asked to tell them about yourself, there it is to guide you. You will eliminate one of the most stressful questions and by the nature of your answer, the flow, the confident tone and the succinctness of your answer will impress them. It will be expressed in a way that facilitates their notes, and by its nature you sound like you know who you are, and how to deliver it. By contrast, your competition is stammering and faking it through this highly dreaded question, and you are coming out in front right from the start.

This is also where the Skills Alignment Matrix will come in to up your game. You have both the employer's needs and your alignment with the position right in front of you. No need to scramble and search for anything. To strengthen your position and to help the interviewer pass on your value to others, offer to email the Skills Alignment Matrix as you speak. This will prove to be a powerful means of communicating your value as well as demonstrating your professionalism and creativity in putting together business documents.

The phone is the launching pad to the face to face. By the nature of its limitations in communication, it can either help or hinder you. If you recall how effective and natural you were using the the phone when gainfully employed, dealing with a multitude of issues day in and day out, you can recapture that spirit and thrive in that environment. Take it for what it is, a means to set up an appointment. Use the tools explained to sharpen your conversation skills, build confidence, and get you closer to meeting your prospects for a face to face meeting.

CHAPTER 51

EVERY INTERVIEW QUESTION IS YOUR STAGE— SHOW IT, DON'T TELL IT!

Prior to the interview, if you have only presented the traditional resume, traditional cover letter, and an application, *you are only a one dimensional figure to those interviewing you.* The materials you have provided them— through the very nature of their limited scope—demonstrate only a small percentage of your full potential.

Even if you have presented the cover letter, Professional Profile, Skills Alignment Matrix and other materials referred to in this book, you still have to strengthen your case and hence their knowledge of you by creating an exciting, compelling and memorable picture of you in their heads. It's your job to take their one-dimensional perception of you and turn it into an amazing display of all your talents and value.

Think of the interview process as a surgical operation to the interviewer. Figuratively speaking, they would love to cut you open to find out what's really going on in your head. Can you do the job? Are you going to stick around? Are you really all you say you are? Are you sane? They would love to know it all.

That's where the questions come in. Relevant or irrelevant. Questions that probe about your last job. Scenario based questions. Behavioral type questions. Questions that seem wildly insane and obviously have nothing to do with the interview. One thing for certain, you can never anticipate what questions will be asked. So how can you prepare for them?

Think of every interview question as your stage; your opportunity to demonstrate who you are, what you are, what you have done, and your stage to display many of the amazing accomplishments over the span of your career.

This is where your real life stories and situations are the key to transforming you from a one-dimensional figure on a piece of paper to a 3D powerhouse, in living color.

All those terrific accomplishments you wanted to put on paper but couldn't, here's the chance. All the great ways you closed a deal, wooed that 'impossible' client, created the advertising piece that generated millions of dollars, this is your time to put it on display.

We all have stories to tell from our careers that excite and create interest. Take some time and hone a half dozen of them to be able to tell them with succinctness and enthusiasm. Give them flesh and blood. Expand upon the names, numbers, who, what, where. Make them exciting, and make them count.

When you are asked a question, any question, do your best to use these stories to bring you to life. Make yourself memorable. Talk about the incredible things they'd never know about you—unless you personally tell them.

When you tell your story, tell it in 3 parts. : (1) What was the situation. (2) What actions did you take and (3) what was the *awesome* outcome. Keep in mind, as you are telling the story, you are *also* filling them in on all kinds of other things about you that will add value to your credibility.

Don't just say "When I was working on a project in China..." Instead say "I was head engineer on a $200 million project in Shanghai, one of many I had spearheaded globally..."

Don't just say "I handled a difficult client by addressing their needs by asking a lot of questions." Instead tell them, as one job seeker did "As Branch Manager of a $125 million deposit branch, in an area of high profile celebrities, I found myself sitting across from a member of one of the wealthiest and most well known families in America, a Kennedy..."

In the end, the question may not even matter compared to all the 'other' things you end up saying that demonstrates to them that you should be hired—now!

Every interview question is your stage. Use it to your advantage. Perform and blow your horn!

CHAPTER 52

THE CONSULTATIVE INTERVIEW—WHAT ARE THEIR NEEDS?

When you go to the doctor, the first question he asks you is "What seems to be the problem?" When you sit down with a consultant the first thing he inquires about is "How can I help you?".

Turn the tables on the interview process and start thinking of yourself as a doctor or a consultant. Your job is to help them with their problems. In order to be able to help the company, you need to know all about their challenges and pending needs.

Interviewers seemingly fail to understand that the point in hiring you is to fill a need the company has and to solve their problems. They 'interview' candidates with a barrage of questions that often have little or nothing to do with the problems the company is facing. Then from these questions they some how derive the fact that you're a good or a bad fit.

Start approaching every interview as if you were a consultant and focus in on asking those questions that will bring to light the challenges and needs of the company; then address those needs by demonstrating how you managed such similar problems in your previous job. Aligning as closely as possible what you did before with *their needs* can be very powerful in painting a picture that shows them you are a great candidate to consider.

Following this method you will find yourself far more in control, and you will find that the interview will become more of a professional dialogue between 'professionals' and not an interview that seemingly goes nowhere and never addresses what the job is really all about.

Always keep in mind, the point of every interview is to simply find out what the needs of the company are and to demonstrate how you can be the solution to these needs. Be the consultant and watch the tables turn in your favor.

CHAPTER 53

DEALING WITH SPEED BUMPS

Some questions tend to haunt you even before they are asked. Why did you lose your last job? Why did you only stay here for 5 months? What's this 6-month gap? These are what are referred to as 'speed bumps'—and that's all they are—minor questions they can be quickly and succinctly answered, then move on.

The problem arises when we transform them into a seemingly Mt. Everest before we even start the interview. Instead of focusing in on how we are going to help the company, we are thinking about how we are going to deal with these questions that have absolutely nothing to do with the position at all. We exasperate ourselves by putting undue importance on these questions until they become the focal point of the interview in our minds; instead of showcasing who we are, what we have accomplished and what we have to offer the company.

The approach here is to realize they are just minor speed bumps. Answer them with a succinct answer and move on. Do not try and come up with an answer that can be perceived any different number of ways. Don't come across in an apologetic manner trying to explain your way out. This is dangerous, as you never know how it is being perceived, and it just may take you right out of the game.

Here are some effective responses: "There was organizational restructuring and my position was eliminated." "Another opportunity surfaced that aligned with my expertise far better." "Looking for work was a challenging period, for sure, but I took the opportunity to hone my Excel skills, network, attend industry specific seminars and increase my exposure through community service".

One client, the regional manager of a large retail chain, had been out of work for 9 months before meeting him for a private session. His problem wasn't getting interviews; his problem was he was not getting past Human Resources in the interviews, and he had no idea why. Then I asked him why he left his last job.

"I met my wife there. She was a cashier. We started dating and 6 months later we got married. When the company heard about this, we were both unfairly terminated."

I then explained to him that this was the culprit that was keeping him unemployed. What he was saying, and what Human Resources was deriving from what he was saying were two different perspectives. He saw it as an unfair termination. Human Resources saw him as a guy who wasn't concentrating on his work. A manager that was flirting with the staff, and then started dating one of them. Here was a guy who was breaking all the sexual harassment laws, and in fact could be setting them up for a potential sexual harassment suit if they hired him. Red flags all over.

When I explained this to him, and how he should appropriately reply, he was hired after his very next interview. When I talked to him afterwards, I asked how it went. He replied, "Without a hitch! I can't believe I had been answering that question with that answer, even though I knew all about sexual harassment. This time I just told them I was let go due to some changes, period".

Don't allow speed bump questions to unnerve you. Take them for what they are, and when you do answer them, reply succinctly and with an answer that isn't going to raise flags. Then move on.

CHAPTER 54

TURNING AN INTERVIEW INTO A DIALOGUE

If an interview is turning into an interrogation, (and you'll know it when it starts becoming a stream of questions shooting from the interviewer, and all you are doing is responding and probably feeling uncomfortable) don't blame the interviewer, blame yourself.

Keep in mind, most interviewers, from recruiters to Human Resources to Decision Makers, are not good at interviewing. They are not sure what to ask, so they ask a lot of questions hoping to find out all about you. They are often uncomfortable with the process, and may even appear nervous. Many of their questions have come from the internet, and they have no idea why they are even asking them. Obviously "What is your favorite fruit?" has nothing to do with the job unless you are perhaps an expert on taste.

The key to this is turning their questions into dialogues. This can be done by following their questions with a response that requires a response from them. Then respond back with questions that are focused on the company—and what their needs are.

Interviewer: "Can you tell us about some one of your weaknesses?"

You: Tell them a specific story about a weakness of yours you have overcome and follow up your response with "May I ask what are some of the challenges you are facing and working to overcome in your department?"

Of course you have to handle this situation with extreme business acumen and sensitivity to the personality of the interviewer. Be aware of the ebb and flow of the dialogue. Handle it as a professional in a professional setting. Use tact and strategically get your questions in.

If you find your next interview turning into an interrogation, don't yield to it. Help them help themselves; and you by focusing in on their needs.

CHAPTER 55

LISTENING— TURNING THE TABLES IN YOUR FAVOR

During the entire course of the interview, your most effective tool is your ability to listen.

If you are approaching the interview as a consultant, to find out their needs, you better be good at it, as a good consultant listens far more than he speaks

In the business world, people and companies keep their cards close to their chest. It takes some probing, and some intense listening on your end to pick up cues about their real needs and pains. We are all motivated either by the need to alleviate pain or to seek gain. Given that, questions that probe in those areas are the key to finding out their needs, and may even reveal needs they were unaware of having.

Yet all the questioning in the world will be futile, if instead of intense listening on your end, you are making mental notes (or scribbling notes in your notepad), and focusing on those areas you can align your skills and accomplishments with; you are starting to 'think' and lose focus on what *they* saying because you are pondering a comeback to their response.

Listening is a bit of a dance; between picking up jewels you can use in your favor, filing them away very quickly, (while continuing on letting them speak)—without formulating your answer, *which stops you from listening,* if only for a few seconds—which could be a few seconds of such importance you missed a major opportunity.

It seems to be our natural instinct to want to burst into a conversation when we find ourselves aligning perfectly with a particular issue or problem someone is relating to us. Resist that urge. There is plenty of time to express ourselves later in the interview. The key here is listening, clearing our minds, picking up those points we can use to strengthen our cause, and show the interviewer we have the capacity to give them our full and undivided attention; which even that alone, will earn us strong points as you move through the interview process.

CHAPTER 56

SO DO YOU HAVE ANY QUESTIONS?

Typically near the end of the interview you will be asked if you have any questions. If you haven't done so already, this is the place to turn the interview around to what it should have been in the first place—a dialogue about the their needs and how you can address them.

I have heard countless stories of job seekers turning interviews around in their favor and even taking control of the interview by simply asking questions such as:

- What specifically are you looking for in the ideal candidate?
- What are some of your biggest challenges?
- What is keeping you up at night?
- What specific needs do you have that are not on the job description?
- What can I do within the first 3 months to make the biggest impact to the company?

One job seeker had been to 10 interviews and failed them all. On his 11th after the interview was wrapping up after only 30 minutes, he inquired about some of the biggest challenges the company faced.

"The entire atmosphere of the room changed. The interviewers started getting excited and begin spilling things about the company that had nothing to do with the job description at all. I listened and countered with similar problems at other companies I had worked at, and they loved it!" The interview then went on for another 90 minutes. Needless to say he landed the job.

Another interviewer had asked Human Resources before an interview if there were any specific needs of the marketing team that were not on the job description. Human Resources replied that the Chief Marketing Officer had mentioned "Change'" a number of times, but she had no idea what he had meant; "Whatever that's all about?"

Seeing this as an opportunity, the job seeker asked the CMO at the conclusion of the interview what was their biggest challenge.

"It was amazing." Explained the interviewee "The Chief Marketing Officer's body language and demeanor changed completely. He became very passionate and went on for 10 minutes about the massive changes in the banking world and that if they don't change they will all be finished!"

The interviewee countered with all the changes at a previous company he had worked and how he was instrumental in bringing about change. This led to further dialogue and the interview went on for nearly 2 hours. He also noted that "I thought it interesting that the Chief Marketing Officer was so adamant about change yet the head of Human Resources was oblivious to it." Another example that Human Resources is usually out of touch with the real needs of decision makers.

So ask questions—which is what the interview should be all about in the first place. What are the needs of the company, what is their pain, what do they want to gain, and what specifically are they looking for to solve their problems? Simple, effective and powerful.

CHAPTER 57

STAY IN CONTROL BY ASKING CLOSING QUESTIONS

As the interview winds down, you want to position yourself in a place that puts you in as much control as possible. The following questions can help you do just that; from leveraging one interview to the next, to knowing where you are in the interview process; letting you know if you should soldier on or put the prospect behind you and look for better opportunities—and there will *always* be better opportunities.

1. ***What are the next steps?*** Just as you inquired about who will be interviewing you for the first interview, *it is imperative you find out about the subsequent interviews.* Who will be interviewing you? What will that interview entail? You may be surprised how open people are to share this information with you. Remember it is in *their* best interest for you to shine in subsequent interviews. Those passing you on will now have a vested

interest in you, as it now becomes a reflection of them. So always ask what the next steps will be so you will be prepared for what is to follow.

2. *What is your timeframe in selecting someone?* There is nothing quite so frustrating as leaving an interview and being kept in the dark regarding when they will be making a selection. In asking this question you will know when you can follow up and either move to the next step or put it to bed and move on. It will keep you in control of the process, eliminate any anxiety in waiting and allow you to keep a clear mind to continue other endeavors. It also demonstrates your business acumen. Just as when you were working, you always worked within a timeframe to keep business flowing smoothly. Use that same professionalism now in the interview process.

3. **When will you be reaching out to me about your decision/second interview, etc?** By asking this question, you will eliminate that dreaded waiting period that follows an interview. Countless times I have been asked by job seekers 'When should I make a followup call to my last interview?' I respond by telling them that if they haven't called you by the time they said they would, call them. This question will keep you in control of the process and if you are approaching the interview as a 'consultant,' it will be a natural flow in the course of your dialogue.

CHAPTER 58

TURNING A FOLLOW-UP INTO AN OFFER

When following up on an interview, keep in mind that the company is also going through a difficult period in trying to select the best candidate. That the company is not 'in the business of hiring' and they may be very much in the dark as well. They may believe they have done a great job in the selection process, but with bad hires rampant, and with a couple of bad hires already under their belt, they also know they are taking a risk with every hire.

Be empathetic with them. Let them know you sympathize with them about trying to find the best candidate for the job.

Inquire whether they have found a candidate that has met all their needs. More often than not they may respond that they are still looking or have narrowed it down to a few hopefuls. Ask them what they are looking for in the perfect candidate but have not yet found. You may be surprised what they say, and it may give you the information to move *their* selection process in *your* favor.

This is also the time, if you have not already submitted it, to let them know you have put together a Skills Alignment Matrix that precisely aligns your skills and expertise with the needs of their job description. Give it to them there and then or either email it to them immediately after the interview. This has been proven numerous times to tip the scales in the candidate's favor, and lead to an offer.

Don't underestimate the power of slowly and incrementally tipping the scales in your favor by providing additional materials that demonstrate your excellent fit for the job.

A highly accomplished insurance executive had been out of work for 5 months when she was interviewed for a 'dream job'. Four interviews later she was confident she was going to get an offer. Then she came into my office distraught. "They hired someone else!" she exclaimed nearly in tears. Knowing how good of a candidate she was, I became personally vested in her search.

"Create a Skills Alignment Matrix and send it to the CFO" I told her. "Somebody has to see how perfect you are for the job!"

She went home, created it and sent it off in a hand written addressed, stamped envelope to the CFO. A few days later she received a call from Human Resources that they wanted to see her again.

"When I showed up for the interview on Friday, the CFO actually had my folded Skills Alignment Matrix in her hand. She commented on how she loved it and how well I aligned with the job. The interview went great! The next day, 10:00 a.m. Saturday morning I received a call and they made me an offer for a higher position in the company. The offer was *more* than I was making at my previous job in NYC!"

The effectiveness of turning a follow-up into an offer depends considerably on your ability to find out more precisely the employer's 'wish list' for the perfect candidate, demonstrating with the Skills Alignment Matrix how well you address their needs, and incrementally turning the tables in your favor by creating powerful tools that will win them over to your favor.

CHAPTER 59

THE OFFER—WHAT ARE YOUR SALARY EXPECTATIONS?

"What are your salary expectations?"

No matter how it is framed or who it is asked of—this question can put even the most seasoned professional into a tailspin. It seems no matter how skilled one may be in the art of negotiation, when you find yourself unemployed, ostensibly with very little leverage, and that job floating out there like a life saver out of reach in a turbulent sea, suddenly all your skills at negotiating fall by the wayside.

Since you were a child we have heard the saying "He who speaks first loses" yet there in the midst of the interview you are suddenly spouting out a salary number. With Human Resources looking on, there you sit, worrying if you say too much, they will throw up their hands and say, "Too much! Interview over!" Like a baseball player in the World Series last inning, bases full hearing the umpire scream "You're Out!"

One new Job Club member had been making $110,000 when he was let go. In a panic, he and his wife had determined they could get by on $65,000 (roughly 60% of his previous salary). When asked at the end of the second interview how much he was looking for, he replied "I'll need at least $65,000." The interviewer in turn replied "Well, we had actually budgeted a lot more for this position." The candidate later accepted the offer at $67,500, leaving according to his calculations, $30k to $40k on the table. Ugh!

Before we go into how to counter this question, let's first explore the dynamics and perceptions of the offer.

First of all, if they are making an offer, remember that they *really* want you. This means that you do *have* leverage. They've expended the resources to bring you this far in the process, a number of people have agreed on the decision, and they are forming a vested interest in you. Taking into consideration the 'maximum' as to what they can offer you, they will do whatever it takes to get you— they just don't want you to know this—so lose the fear of asking what you are worth.

I have personally closed very large gaps between employers and candidates when the gaps in perceivable terms seemed insurmountable. A banker making $86,000 yet accepting $55,000 once understanding the 'whole compensation package'. A company paying out $78,000 when the top base salary had been frozen at $53,000 for 3 years. A Communications Executive accepting $175,000 when she had been making $350,000.

In all of these cases, *an examination of the entire compensation package, the actual value the candidate was bringing on board and/or the prospects of opportunity and growth bridged the gap between the parties.*

If ever a highly sought after candidate has requested too much, I have rarely seen an employer scoff it off and declare "Game over!" They will continue in the process, exhausting all means, until they have reached their ceiling. Never forget, if they have made you an offer, *they want you!* They may not be able to pay you what you want, but they want you. That is leverage.

Secondly, your purpose in the interview is to demonstrate your value. The more value you can demonstrate to the employer, the more leverage you have in getting a more robust compensation package. It can be very powerful to reiterate the value you are bringing on board. The more marbles you bring to the game, the more you should be compensated. If you can manage a team, excel at all the technical skills required, and are a top closer—you are bringing a lot more to the table than just being a manager with technical skills.

When asked "How much?" You need to be thinking "What's the deal?" It's *not* just about a bottom line salary figure. Get that out of your head. You need to know what the entire compensation package is all about.

Many times I have told people I am personal friends with some very wealthy people with 5 children. I mention they are looking for a nanny to care for their kids for one year and they are willing to write out a check for $1,000,000 in advance. This sounds like an infinite amount of money in a one lump sum, right? Almost everyone wants to sign up for the job. Then when I tell them, traveling with the kids, flights, hotels, meals etc., will be all on their dime, they shake their heads and turn it down. Of course they do, they'll go broke. $1,000,000 really is a finite amount of money.

The point of the story is, it's not what you make up front, *it's what you put in your pocket at the end of the day* that counts. Herein lies the danger of concentrating on a salary number, and not on the entire compensation package.

So tell them "I'm really interested in the whole compensation package." "That once you review that, you are confident you can both come to an agreement on the base salary."

This puts everything in proper perspective. What are you getting? If you are getting a base of $80,000 but are paying $1,000 in benefits a month, you are really making $68,000. If you are required to put out $500 a month on travel expenses above what they are offering you, there's another $6,000, bringing it down to $62,000 (See the Compensation Grid in Chapter 63 to determine what you are really bringing home).

It's actually quite amazing that figuring out how much you will be making after the 'expenses' of the job, is usually the last thing people think about. When determining your salary, make it the first thing you think about.

If they continue on demanding a number from you, ask them "what's the range?", then go for the top number, or the number you feel you are worth. If the top range is $130,000 and you were making $90,000, then perhaps you should consider aiming a little lower. Use your professional acumen at this stage.

Negotiating your salary can be a nerve wrecking experience. Avoid throwing out numbers at random. Put it into perspective that this is a business transaction. Keep our focus on the entire compensation package and not just a base figure. Do our numbers so we know what we are netting at the end of the day, we will more effectively and with more credibility be able to negotiate a compensation package more favorable to us.

CHAPTER 60

THE COMPENSATION GRID

The Compensation Grid is a powerful tool in determining the true value of the compensation package.

The following is an actual grid that was used to compare two offers received by a candidate. He was offered $82,000 from XYZ, CO and $70,000 from ABC, CO.

At first he instinctively was going to accept the $82,000 offer. Yet in using the grid to calculate what he was actually going to be 'netting' from each job, he realized the lower base paying job was actually going to give him $5000+ more!

"After doing the grid, it became a no brainer!" he remarked, and accepted the lower paying job.

The grid has also been very effective in justifying to employers 'why' you need more compensation. It rationally lays out the numbers and gives you justification for asking for more. Thus avoiding the 'auction style' compensation game that employers tend to use by throwing you an additional few thousand dollars (without any rhyme or reason) hoping to close the deal.

In using the grid, simply plug in your base salary and list your expenses. Also include any bonus structure, 401k plans, etc., they may substantially impact the bottom line.

You may be very surprised to find the job that ostensibly pays less up front, is actually putting more in your pocket at the end of the day!

Compensation Grid

ABC vs XYZ Corp Annual Costs and Net EArnings Based on 52 Work Weeks

Annual Expenses	ABC	XYZ
Base	70,000.00	82,000.00
Tax @ 25%	-17,500.00	-20,500.00
Car Maint. & Wear/Tear @ 200 per month	0.00	-2,400.00
Gas @ 2.20/60 RT Miles @ 20mpg	0.00	-1,666.50
Tolls	0.00	-1,893.75
401K Retirement Plan 6% Employer Contribution	4,200.00	0.00
Health/Life Insurance Cost	0.00	-3,600.00
Parking	0.00	-720.00
Net	56,700.00	51,219.75

CHAPTER 61

ACCEPTING THE OFFER AND NEGOTIATING FOR MORE

Congratulations! You've received an offer! But the game isn't over yet.

Unless the offer is everything you wanted and the details were already worked out in advance, resist the urge to accept it then and there. Yes, express your gratitude and thanks for the offer and how excited you are to be welcomed into their team; yet realize that this is also a period that you just may be able to negotiate for more that may result in substantial benefits later down the road.

After you have expressed your thanks for the offer, ask them if you can get back to them the next day, or perhaps the following Monday to confirm your acceptance. Of course Human Resources doesn't want to hear this, as they would rather put the hire to rest. *But the job isn't about them now, it's about you, your needs.*

Allowing time for you to gather your thoughts, settle back with a clear objective mind, and analyze a job that may consume years of your life, is crucial. Do your numbers. Have you plugged into the compensation grid, what you will be putting in your pocket at the end of the day? Or have you blindly accepted a base figure with no thought of expenses? Have you considered the cost for benefits? Will the schedule they have given you work? Does the vacation time allow you to attend that family gathering you have planned every year?

This time more than any other time throughout the entire process, is finally the time for you to have some leverage—and it could be very powerful leverage.

In negotiating for more and better compensation, there are entire books written on this subject. One of the major key points to keep in mind is to avoid becoming emotional. It's easy with a new offer to allow your emotions to take over, and to accept less, fearing that you just may lose the opportunity if you attempt to negotiate for more. Fight the urge to become emotional by reminding yourself that this is simply another business transaction. Emotions are your enemy in negotiations and they cloud your clarity of thinking; the other party, the company, is not getting bogged down with emotional thoughts, and neither should you. Stay calm and stay focused.

The simplest way to test where they stand with the offer is to ask upon *receiving* it, "Is there any financial flexibility in the whole compensation package?" Almost inevitably they will respond with something like, "I'm sorry, we've reached our ceiling," or "Perhaps, there may be some room." Human Resources, will generally know the limit, they just don't want you to know. Take note that this question is a "yes" or "no" type question. All we want to know is if they will consider amendments to the offer.

If you feel they have genuinely reached their ceiling on the base, ask about reviews. Ask when they are and what are they based upon. You may be surprised to learn they are based on a monetary reward after say 6 months. If you don't need the health benefits, find out if you can be compensated monetarily by opting out of them.

When it comes to vacation and PTO—Paid Time Off— many companies have a strict policy with incoming employees. Yet, if they have decided they sincerely want you, you just may be surprised.

A credit analyst I had been working with, when made an offer requested an additional 5 days of vacation. Paid or not, he didn't care, all that mattered was he needed the time off. However, the bank that had made the offer had a strict policy that incoming employees were allowed only two weeks off for the first two years. This was the bank's policy and couldn't be changed. Then a creative solution was worked out by a quick thinking Director of Human Resources. It was decided the new employee's Supervisor would approve an additional five days for the first two years of his employment. He then happily accepted the job.

Even if there may not seem much room for negotiation, don't give up. Avoid making it all about the base salary, and look for other factors that may make the offer more attractive. Can they compensate you for your cell phone? Can you get your commuting expenses deducted from your paycheck pre-tax?

If they respond, that there is room for negotiation, then make your request. This is again where the Compensation Grid can come in as a very powerful tool. You can counter with figures that make financial sense. It's the norm for both company and candidate to respond with a bump in salary here, and a bump in salary there, as if they are in an auction. Avoid this with the Compensation Grid. Now you can respond with numbers, backed with actual figures that make your counteroffer entirely legitimate.

Avoid the tendency to be greedy when making a counteroffer and remember that there are limitations. Think creatively. Make a list of your needs and wants. Go assertively after your needs, and attempt to get your wants. Always keep in mind though, you may have to make some compromises in the beginning. Yet, when you are made the offer, remember you will not be given such an opportunity for discussing compensation again for quite a while. What you get from the start may greatly benefit you in years to come.

CHAPTER 62

REFERENCES—SET THE STAGE

I was asking a client about an offer he had received and the topic of discussion turned to references. "When was the last time you spoke to this reference" I inquired.

"Five years ago" she responded.

"Well, a lot can happen in five years, maybe you should call them" I said.

She did call and found the person had left the position the year before and had moved away with no forwarding contact information.

How often do we continue to use the same references without following up on their status? Furthermore, and just as important, how often do we list references without knowing exactly what they are going to say about us?

Just as you are not a professional job seeker, don't make the mistake of thinking your reference is skilled in being a great reference giver or remembers your wonderful qualities. In fact some references could harm you. Instead of letting the caller know you worked there and were a great addition to to the team, they could be sidetracked into talking about your weaknesses that could sabotage your offer.

Contact any and all references you plan to provide and ask them for permission to use them as a reference. When you have their permission, ask them if they mind sharing how they usually respond when contacted. Listen carefully. This is where you want to ideally have a short coaching session with them. Throw a few questions at them and see what they say. Of course you cannot control what a reference will say, but you can make them aware of questions that could potentially harm you. Also, providing your references with a copy of your Professional Profile will give them some background of your career to serve as discussion bullet points.

However you deal with those that you use as references, make sure they are aware they are being used as references and prepare them so that they are not surprised to receive the phone call. And just as important, find out what they are going to be saying about you. Don't allow a great offer to be derailed by a careless slip of a bad reference giver.

CHAPTER 63

ON-BOARDING—
MAKING THE MOST OF IT
FROM THE START

You've accepted the job, now what? Is it all smooth sailing from here on out? Don't let the enthusiasm for the new job cloud your clarity of thinking. On-boarding successfully can pave the way for a great job, great relations, and a good chance at early promotions. Poor on-boarding can lead to frustration, anxiety and loss of your coveted job.

Like any relationship, you have to 'feel' and 'sense' your way into the dynamics of the other party, and in this case, other parties. Who is going to form early alliances with you? Who is going to potentially sabotage you? Enter every new encounter with a fellow worker positively, yet cautiously. Watch carefully how you are welcomed into the group. Make mental notes, and be observant.

Be humble. As the ancient Chinese saying goes, "Be like water." Water takes the form of any container it is poured into. Be the same. Go with the flow, don't fight it, adapt yourself to each situation as it demands.

One Job Club attendee, Jessica started work as a Sales Manager for a manufacturing plant that had a team of salespeople who had been lifetime employees for over 20+ years. The position was a newly created one, and was not welcomed by the sales team.

She understood the challenges of this position, being the new kid on the block, and having to manage a team of seasoned salespeople that felt they didn't need her. Yet, things never jelled and 3 months later she was out, and the position was eliminated.

What happened? The position should never have been created. If they had hired an entirely new salesforce that welcomed change and new ideas, it may have worked. Yet, in such a hostile environment resistant to change, the chances of success were slim. In retrospect, Jessica realized that unless, she had been given more authority, more support by the President, and the ability to bring on new salespeople, her chances of success would have been very low.

This case is extreme, yet demonstrates that the on-boarding process can be a difficult transitional period that requires extreme care and strategic thinking. Perhaps if Jessica had first come on as a salesperson, proved herself to the group, earned their respect and gained credibility, she would have been readily welcomed by the sales team. Yet as it was presented to her, it was doomed for disaster from the beginning.

An extremely important position to take from the beginning is to create relationships with everyone you meet. From the bottom all the way to the top. The security guard that has been there for 15 years, the receptionist that has been there for 10. That elderly manager of the cafeteria may seem incidental to you, yet forming alliances with him, and showing genuine interest in him, may be priceless. One never knows what dynamics are being played out. Your job is to create warm and friendly relations with everyone.

Be highly sensitive to cliques where exclusions of others is the norm. Watch out for any form of gossip or leanings in that way. You can be sure if someone is ready to gossip to you, they will probably gossip about you later down the road. Be aware of your surroundings, and take note of the interplay between workers.

Memorize everybody's name. From the first day you are taken around to meet your co-workers, make notes of everyone and get their names down. This can be a challenge, yet when it comes time for help and advice, and forming strong relationships, this above all will make a great impression upon everybody you subsequently later meet.

As time goes on, make notes of your accomplishments. This can be extremely helpful 3 to 6 months later when your reviews come up.

Don't be caught trying to remember months of details long after they have passed, get them down so that you can relate them in a business tone when needed.

Avoid being intimidated by those superior to you. Treat them with the respect they deserve, yet hold your own sense of value and importance. Keep in mind, you are the expert in your field. You were hired to do a job. If you demonstrate confidence and professional poise, it will be noticed.

Think of the company as yours. Go above and beyond. If you see a can littering the parking lot, pick it up as you walk by it. If the company sink is messy, wipe it down. If the coffee has run out, make a new pot. This attending to small details will be noticed and applauded.

Thank everyone—even when *you* have been the one to help them. Mark Richards, CEO of the Maryl Group in Hawaii, always went out of his way to thank people—even if he had helped them.

Whenever I would encounter a problem with leasing a space or other matter in commercial real estate, I would go to him for help. At the end of each meeting he was always the first to thank *me*. This made a great impression on me, as well as many others, who learned to follow suit in his footsteps. Thank others even when logic dictates they should be thanking you.

Don't lose site of the fact that you are your own company. As mentioned in Chapter 4 ME, Inc -Your Own Company, you may be on a W2 but you are from a business point of view, simply contracting out your services. Always be thinking, is this good for my business? Never lose site that permanent jobs are quickly becoming a thing of the past. Keeping aware of what's happening in your field of expertise is crucial to staying sharp. Never get too comfortable that you won't explore other opportunities that potentially surface.

Thinking about on-boarding may be the last thing on your mind when you are unemployed. Yet, in as little time as 2 weeks from today, you just may find yourself walking into that new company environment.

There are many factors at play in the role as the new employee; the key is to be acutely aware of your new home away from home. Ease into the company. Be humble. Avoid being the new face with all the ideas. There is plenty of time to prove yourself in the months and years to come. Go slowly and incrementally, and as you transition into the team, you will earn the respect and admiration of others, that will help progress in the company, and succeed.

PART V

TIPS AND STRATEGIES
THAT MAKE THE
JOURNEY EASIER

The Devil is surely in the details. It's the subtle things, the invisible that usually make the biggest difference in our endeavors.

CHAPTER 64

SELF-SABOTAGING YOUR JOB SEARCH

When we lose our jobs, the easiest and most frequently one to blame is the employer. We were the one that was always giving their best; it was the employer who was not keeping their end of the bargain. Yet in story after story from job seekers when asked about their last job, more often than not, there are complaints, red flags and misgivings that surface that allude to the fact that the employee had become disgruntled and negative about the employer long before they were let go.

If this is the case, could it be that the employee was self-sabotaging his job, which led to the loss of it? It takes some brutally honest soul searching to admit this. Could the job have been saved if you had turned around your attitude?

Turning to the job search, it's easy to place the blame on the economy. Applicant tracking systems, Human Resources,

259

inept interviewers, the fact companies are not in the business of hiring, etc. Yet, is it possible you are the one to blame for your lack of interviews? Your lack of offers? In fact, perhaps it is you who are self-sabotaging your current job search, yet are unaware at it?

The following is a non-conclusive list of factors that could be self-sabotaging your job search:

- Poor time management
- Negative feelings
- Poor presentation skills
- Fear of failure and rejection
- Reluctance to get out from behind your computer and be proactive
- Fear of the phone
- Using only traditional resumes with all the self-sabotaging perceptions it presents
- Family and friends
- Poor work environment
- Failure to network, or network effectively
- Failure to generate referrals

The list is endless. With self reflection, you know those areas you need to work on, and the time to start working on them is now.

If your time management is suffering, start restructuring your day to accommodate all you need to do. If you feel your presentation and speaking skills are weak, start signing up for public speaking classes at your local college or attending groups such as Toastmasters, which is a public speaking and leadership training program with chapters internationally. If you aren't networking, visit your local Chambers of Commerce and find out about business networking events you can attend, organizations you can volunteer your time, after hour 'meet and greet' opportunities.

Recognizing and admitting those areas that we are self-sabotaging is the first step in addressing these challenges. Start incrementally working on them, and recognize them for what they are, self generated factors that are holding us back—and that only when we start challenging them and working on them, can we start to defeat them and leave them in the past.

CHAPTER 65

REPLACING SELF-CONSCIOUSNESS WITH SELF-CONFIDENCE

"The consciousness of self is the greatest hindrance to the proper execution of all physical action." Bruce Lee writes in his book *The Tao of Jeet Kune Do.*

When you're employed you take your confidence in your job for granted. You perform naturally. You do what has to be done and you do it. No matter what the task, you perform as a professional. You rarely get befuddled by the process. Even when faced with new and challenging problems, you dive in and get the job done. You have all the self confidence in the world.

Now it's different. You've been thrown into a situation that seems to have no rhyme or reason. All your efforts seem hopelessly in vain. The confidence you had when dealing with the 'working world' is fast evaporating and is replaced with feelings of doubt, fear and inadequacy as you receive one rejection after another; as you fail one interview after another.

All these feelings in turn create a self consciousness that do nothing but stop us from succeeding in our job search.

The solution? Reclaim your professionalism. Recognize this venture for what it is, promoting, marketing and selling a product, which are the services you have to offer.

Sure the target is constantly moving and insanely tough to focus on. Of course the customers (employers) are fickle and don't know precisely what they want. Absolutely the task of creating all your marketing tools and getting them out is arduous and with seemingly no end in sight.

But wasn't that how your job was as well? Yes, you were trained and educated in that career, yet you were still faced with a daily onslaught of challenges, which you performed well and often brilliantly. Why? You were confident. You didn't allow self consciousness to sabotage your efforts.

CHAPTER 66

TIPPING THE SCALES, EVEN WHEN ALL SEEMS LOST

Who companies ultimately hire can be a great mystery. It may make no sense at all why they end up making an offer to the person with less years of experience, less credentials, and less than a perfect fit for the job. If we consider that humans are emotional, irrational and illogical, it may help to understand the mystery of why people make the hiring decisions they do.

Why is it that that taller people, more attractive people and slimmer people have a slight advantage over others in the interview process? That extroverts are generally favored over introverts? That blond hair and blue eyes seems to open more doors? Even if the person is less qualified, they can often make up for this lack of accountability just by their presence and demeanor.

What's going on here? What's this all about? Perceptions. People perceive that someone taller, "attractive" and an extrovert is a better leader. Is better at socializing, and hence is a better fit in the company. Does it make sense? Is it fair? Of course not, but it is the reality of the world we live in, and its impact can be readily seen in the way companies appear to hire.

How can you create perceptions that you are better than the other candidates? How can you tip the scales in your favor? Grasp the reality that people are deeply influenced by what they perceive. If you send in a traditional resume with the traditional cover letter, submitted through a job board, you are doing what nearly all of the other job seekers are doing. Have you created any perceptions that you are different? That you are innovative and imaginative?

Yet, if you follow-up with the Skills Alignment Matrix, personally sent to a Decision Maker, you are tipping the scales in your favor. If you follow-up an interview with a 90 day plan, based on the job description and the interview instead of just a typical 'thank you' email, you tip the scales in your favor. If you have a strong reference contact the company *first* and tell them they highly recommend you and why, you are tipping the scales in your favor.

Start thinking of ways you can tip the scales to your advantage. Sometimes even the slightest, incremental actions you take, can have just enough influence to get you the job, when all seems like a lost cause.

CHAPTER 67

CREATING REFERRALS STRATEGICALLY

It's not what you know but who you know, is as pertinent in the job search as it it is in any other endeavor.

A referral is someone that feels safe and confident enough about you to take the risk of passing you on to the next level; and, it's not all about your technical abilities.

We tend to think of referrals as people we already know, contacts we've already established. Yet, everyday we run into potential referrals. With every phone call we make, with every new person we meet, a potential referral is there. What we do with that coincidental short term relationship will determine whether or not it becomes a valued referral or just another passing acquaintance soon to be forgotten.

The 'tools' covered in this book are specifically designed to both maximize these circumstantial encounters as well as to create encounters that will turn into powerful referrals.

The concept of *reclaiming your professionalism*, instills the same state of mind you had when employed, which in turn enables you to reach out to anyone without the fear or intimidation of being rejected—and hence create referrals.

Using the *Professional Profile* as a follow-up in making an acquaintance (not a resume) to let people know who you are and what you are, creates referrals.

Reaching out and marketing to Decision Makers with a Professional Profile to be passed down to Human Resources from a higher authority, becomes a referral.

Getting the *Skills Alignment Matrix* into the hands of Decision Makers to exemplify your talents and your ability to fill the position, creates referrals.

Writing *powerful, succinct cover letters* that are actually read and generate interviews, in turn creates referrals.

Strategic networking that focuses on *them* rather than you—which in turn makes you memorable and liked, and hence creates a chain of circumstances that gets you recognized, creates referrals.

The following story illustrates the use of many of these tools in cultivating a referral where none previously existed—from a job seeker who perceived himself as very poor at creating referrals—and subsequently led to a dream job that was never even anticipated.

Daniel, a 25-year-old graduate in mathematics and computer programming, and diagnosed on the Autism spectrum, who found most social situations extremely challenging, had been coming to the workshops for nearly a year. He had had numerous interviews even by such firms as Google, yet he was no closer to getting a job. In fact he had become so disillusioned by the job search that he was already planning to go back to college as a full time student, coming to grips that perhaps his only recourse was getting another degree to put off the painful job search for another few years.

During the course of the year, Daniel had been attending numerous seminars in Manhattan on Free Open Ware Software, where he had the opportunity to meet many in the field. Yet, his biggest complaint about himself every week was his inability to socialize with the attendees once the seminars ended.

"I honestly don't know what to say to people when we all meet at a bar after the seminar. I feel foolish and out of place." He expressed to the class.

"Keep in mind Daniel, it's not about you, it's about them. Show genuine interest in those you meet and don't worry about making an impression by showing them how much you know. In fact, don't even talk about yourself." I then explained to him "Just get business cards and follow-up with your Professional Profile the next day so they know who you and what you are".

Daniel then proceeded to follow this practice with great results. His anxiety decreased as it took the burden off the challenge of what he perceived as socializing (talking about oneself) and by showing his genuine interest in others, he became genuinely liked by those he met.

The result? When the Director of IT for a not-for-profit in Manhattan, whom Daniel had met a number of times at the seminars, announced he was resigning from his position, he encouraged Daniel to apply.

Daniel knew he was unqualified for such a role, yet to his astonishment, he was interviewed and hired. He was the first to admit, "this is all about making the referral, as I was 'uniquely unqualified' for the position!"

Start making it your business to meet people.

Referrals can come from anywhere and at anytime. Gasp the fact that you can have all the technical ability in the world, yet the guy with the connections and referrals will more than likely move faster and further ahead. Dale Carnegie says is his best selling book *How to Win Friends and Influence People*, "15% of one's financial success is due to one's technical ability, and about 85% is due to skill in human engineering—to personality and the ability to lead people." Grasp this principle and start making referrals work for you.

CHAPTER 68

JOB FAIRS—MAKING THEM WORK FOR YOU

Most job seekers who go to job fairs are generally pretty disappointed. "I was in and out of there in 15 minutes, what a waste of time" seems to be a common response. "I gave them my resume and they told me to look online, what's the point!"

Yet, there is a strategy that has proven time and time again to be effective in getting their attention, making you stand out, and ultimately resulting in interviews and offers.

Prior to the job fair, find out what companies will be there. Pick 5 or 6 companies that interest you. Don't attempt to hit them all. Then, do some preliminary research on them. Find out who's who in the company. Google news on the company. See what positions they are hiring for. Gather up enough information so that when you do talk to their representatives at their booth, you'll come across as someone who has done their homework.

Dress for the job fair as if it is an interview. Remember you are out to make an impression. Bring along copies of your Professional Profile and your resume. Carry these in a binder. Be professional and business oriented.

When you do meet one of their representatives, and this could be a recruiter for the company, someone from Human Resources, a manager, once again, create an impression. Extend your hand, smile, introduce yourself and ask them how they are doing. Address them by their name (they will be wearing a name tag) and make them feel valued and important. If you are able to start a discussion, do so. Ask them how long they've been with the company. How they like working for the company. Questions about them that will start a dialogue. The object is to get beyond just the preliminary greeting.

Then pull out your resume and Professional Profile. Hand them your resume, and then your Professional Profile. Explain to them what it is. That it's a short professional bio that you've put together to help them in better understanding your key skills and accomplishment without having to wade through the lengthy resume.

If they wish to engage in more conversation, so much the better. If not, inquire about jobs in your capacity. The general protocol at Job Fairs is for them to tell you to keep checking online for upcoming jobs. Let them know you will, then ask for their business card.

Take a moment to read the business card and then tell them "This is great. I will check on line and I will also *keep you in the loop* in case something comes up." This is very important; as now, you have brought them into your circle, included them in your job search and created a referral. Then warmly thank them and move on. If need be write a short note on the back of their business card to remind yourself of the person you met. It is pertinent you remember the person, especially something you may have discussed with them.

That night, and no later than the next day, shoot them off an email, thanking them for their time, and include something you can mention from the discussion you had with them. The point here is to help them recall you from the masses of other people they met. Tell them you have attached your resume and Professional Profile for their records and that you will take their suggestion and keep checking online for any job opportunities with the company; and that you will keep them in the loop if you see something.

This creating a referral when none existed before, with someone within the company can be very powerful.

Then continue to check online. If something comes up of interest, apply to it. Usually in the application they will ask if you know anyone at the company. This is where your contact comes in. Insert their name. Then after applying send your contact another email telling them you took their advice, found a job and applied to it. Then send them the cover letter and resume you submitted.

Following this process has resulted in some excellent results for many job fair attendees, who previously found little value in them. Make job fairs work for you, instead of just another wasted trip ending in frustration.

CHAPTER 69

WHAT IF IT NEVER COMES BACK?

This question is often asked to job seekers in the workshops, and especially to those whose jobs have been outsourced, become obsolete, or they just no longer have the physical energy or ability to do it. Whatever the reason, what if it never comes back? What if at now, say at age 62, you have to start all over again, what can you do?

Many of you reading this, may be looking inwardly and thinking you've put in months, or even years into a job search, only to finally admit to yourself that it isn't coming back. Then, of course, it's time to turn things around and start looking into other opportunities.

When many participants in our workshops finally come to this conclusion, *and* start inwardly looking, it is amazing to hear and see changes of tremendous opportunity that never surfaced before.

Rebecca, a legal secretary and paralegal for nearly 30 years, tried unsuccessfully for 5 months to get back into a law firm. Yet every door was closed to her. She was either too qualified. Too limited. Too this and too that. Truth be known, she was also entirely burnt out on the profession, and this was probably coming through in the interviews. So she finally gave up and started brainstorming. After some questioning about her real passions in life, suddenly things took a 180 degree turn. Suddenly this shy, quiet woman in class, transformed into an accomplished public speaker, and fearless advocate for local politics. When quizzed further, she revealed she had been involved in politics for years on a local level. The contacts she had, and the knowledge of how the political system operated were extensive. As of this writing, she is making inroads into establishing a political career by running in local politics.

Fritz, a Project Manager and owner of his own construction company found himself at 72 unemployed. He was able to land a few temporary jobs but they both ended very quickly. Then month after month he kept sending out resumes with very little to show for it. He was starting to get very discouraged and talked of finally giving up. He then heard of a civil service exam for facilities maintenance, and decided to take the test. To his astonishment he scored in the top 3%! Soon he was getting calls from all over the state for interviews and landed a job with a school district with a salary of what he was making in his peak years with his own company.

As the saying goes, "It ain't over till it's over" and with support, encouragement and faith, it's only a matter of time until something happens to turn things around—but you must continue to be creative, research alternative careers that align with your key skills and accomplishments and it's advisable to make contact with an experienced and proven career counselor who will be able to objectively review your talents and recommend a strategic plan.

PART VI

THE BEGINNING OF A GREAT ADVENTURE

CHAPTER 70

THE CHALLENGE

At the outset we likened losing your job to facing open heart surgery, leaving you with no direction. The journey through the world of unemployment can be long and hard.

Having read this book, here is the challenge:

Now that you have proven, non-conventional tools, techniques and strategies at your fingertips, what will you do? You have within the pages of this book the tools and strategies to put your life on a positive trajectory to landing your dream job.

We challenge you to:

- Relinquish the passive, highly unproductive 'one size fits all' methods of the traditional job search and start from this moment to launch a proactive campaign to market yourself and find an employer who recognizes you are the solution to their needs.

- Accept the fact that employers are 'not in the business of hiring' and thus need your help to help them realize you are a 'best fit' for their company.

- Reclaim your professionalism by grasping the truth that all your years of education, training and work experience didn't evaporate overnight with unemployment. From this moment you will conduct yourself in everything you do as the professional you are; from the way you think, speak, people you interact with, materials you present, confidence you behold, clothes you wear—the exact same persona you possessed prior to your unemployment.

- Start reaching out to Decision Makers at every opportunity you have; uncover them, contact them, speak to them, make appointments with them—just as you did when you were employed.

- Stop reaching out to 'non decision makers' as the answer to your unemployment problems. You didn't when you were employed, so don't do it now.

- Establish yourself as a company unto yourself (ME, Inc.) and take an assertive, objective stance at this business venture of finding a job.

- Make it a priority to reach beyond the empty seat mentality, and trust that companies are always hiring the best of the best.

- Immediately start creating your Professional Profile, to succinctly present who you are and what you have to offer to both yourself and potential employers.

- Adopt the mindset that it's not all about you; it's all about their needs and how you can meet them.

- Create the right resume for *you*, that highlights your strengths and showcases positive perceptions of you—and negates those negative perceptions that keep doors closed.

- Start writing cover letters that are powerful, address the needs of the job description and are get read … not just glanced over.

- Showcase your talents by preparing a Skills Alignment Matrix.

- Discipline yourself by establishing a consistent, uninterrupted daily work schedule to allow quality time for work search activities.

- Start generating more and better referrals by using great marketing materials as keys that open doors to opportunities, and by using networking acumen that makes your referrals 'want to help you'.

- Track your job search as you would any marketing database.

- Wow interviewers with your awesome marketing materials, so that you take charge of the interview and command favorable job offer terms.

- Use every interview question as a stage for you to demonstrate who you are and what you have to offer—far beyond the one dimensional resume.

- Create the Compensation Grid to determine in realistic and practical terms what your compensation really means.

- Coach yourself to stand strong in dealing with compensation issues and realize it's about the entire compensation package—not just a base figure.

- Become a member of the Job Club and realize that you have a choice 'going it alone' in the job search or joining hands with others and through such concerted efforts expanding your chances of success exponentially.

**Your job search destiny is now in your hands.
Powerful tools are now in your hands.**

To be, or not to be, that is the question:
Whether 'tis nobler in the mind to suffer
The slings and arrows of outrageous fortune,
Or to take arms against a sea of troubles,
And by opposing end them.
—William Shakespeare

YOU'RE NOT ALONE

Perhaps the hardest part of the job search is it's such a lonely process. Gathering up the initiative to tackle the job search takes reaching deep inside and making a conscious effort to forge ahead. Sitting down and creating the marketing materials that are the keys to your success takes time; a lot of time to get them right. Keeping up the momentum when all seems against you requires even more energy, especially if you try to do it all alone.

We are here for you throughout the process; all you have to do is ask. Our one on one personal coaching is focused on you taking control of your job search, and provides the following:

- Coaching and counseling to get you mentally prepped and armed to face the job search with confidence and faith in yourself and your endeavors.
- Formulate together a personal job search plan that holds you accountable and jumpstarts the job search process.

- Review of all your marketing materials and constructive critique to get them tight and right.

- One on one interview prepping. Don't blow the job of a lifetime because you decided to go it alone, and fake it till you make it!

- At your fingertips advice through texting us about immediate issues that need answers NOW! You're negotiating an offer and you need some quick answers, you're nervous before an interview and need some fast confidence, you're sending in a thank you letter and need a quick review, etc., we are here for you.

- Call us at (646)-801-JOBS to discuss a customized plan to fit your career and job search needs.

Visit our websites to stay abreast of job search strategies and become a member of the Breakthrough Job Club:

www.breakthroughjobcoach.com

www.mobile.twitter.com/btjobcoach

Facebook.com/Breakthroughjobcoach.com

71856815R00172

Made in the USA
Middletown, DE
30 April 2018